The
NATIONAL PARKS
and Other Wild Places of
THAILAND

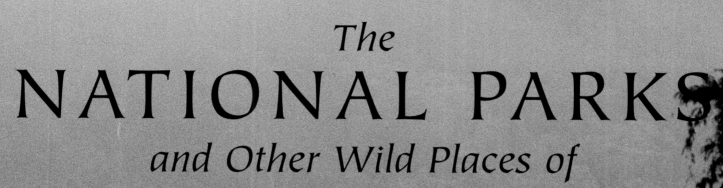

The
NATIONAL PARKS
and Other Wild Places of
THAILAND

Text by Stephen Elliott
Photographs by Gerald Cubitt

ASIA BOOKS

Published and distributed by
Asia Books Co., Ltd.
5 Sukhumvit Road, Soi 61
PO Box 40, Bangkok 10110, Thailand
Tel: (66 2) 715-9000 ext. 3202-4
Fax: (66 2) 714-2799
email: information@asiabooks.com
Website: www.asiabooks.com

2 4 6 8 10 9 7 5 3 1

ISBN 1 85974 886 4

Publishing Manager: Jo Hemmings
Series Editor: Mike Unwin
Project Editor: Camilla MacWhannell
Copy Editor: Tim Sharrock
Cover Design: Alan Marshall
Designer: Stonecastle Graphics Ltd
Cartography: William Smuts
Production: Joan Woodroffe

Reproduction by Pica Digital Pte Ltd, Singapore
Printed and bound in Singapore by Star Standard Industries (Pte) Ltd

Publishers' Note
Throughout this book, species are, where possible, referred to by their
common rather than their scientific names for ease of reference by the general
reader. Where no common names exist, scientific names are used. Many of
the titles listed in the further reading section on page 172 provide full
scientific names for species found in Thailand. The maps contained in the
book are intended as 'locators' only; detailed, large-scale maps should be
consulted when planning a trip. It is important to note that access,
accommodation, and other details vary as new transport methods and
facilities develop. Remember that trail routes can vary, river courses can
change, and water depths can alter dramatically within minutes. Although the
publishers and author made every effort to ensure that the information in this
book was correct at the time of going to press, they accept no responsibility
for any loss, injury or inconvenience sustained by any person using the book.

Map legend for section maps
shown between pages 20 and 166

23	Other highway	Park HQ ▣	General information
551	Main road	*Nong Yom Waterfall* ●	Place of interest
	Secondary road	*Mae Nam Pai*	Water feature
	Track	Khao 743m Salak Phet ▲(2438ft)	Peak in metres (feet)
MALAYSIA	International boundary	✈	International airport
- - - - - - -	Protected Area boundary	✦	Other airport
Chiang Mai ◎	City or major town	⌂	Lodge
Takuapa ◎	Village or small town	⋀	Campsite

Illustrations appearing in the preliminary pages are as follows:
Half title: Tiger; Title pages: Dawn at Phu Khieo Wildlife Sanctuary; Pages
4–5: Limestone karst north of Surat Thani, Southern Thailand; Pages 6–7:
Limestone outcrops, Krabi; Pages 8–9: Long-tailed Macaques congregate in
Phetchaburi Province.

CONTENTS

FOREWORD

Thailand is home to some of the richest biological resources in the world, even though it covers a relatively small total area of 513,115 km². 20–25 percent of the country is covered with forest, peat swamp forest and mangrove forest, and 2,600 km of coastline face the South China Sea to the east and the Andaman Sea on the west side. About one-third of the coastal areas are bordered by mangrove forests. However, during the past few decades of unsustainable development, Thailand has lost large areas of habitat and innumerable wildlife species as a result of deforestation. In the past, over 70 percent of the total land area was covered with various kinds of tropical forest.

Today, our tropical forests support some 15,000 species of vascular plants, roughly 16,000 known species of animals and about 10,000 known species of micro-organisms. It is believed that more than 100,000 species of living organisms in the tropical forests of Thailand are undiscovered; and it is research into the identification of these unknown species that The Biodiversity Research and Training Program (BRT) currently supports.

Huay Kha Khaeng and Thung Yai Naresuan Wildlife Sanctuaries, which have been designated as a "World Heritage Site" by UNESCO, are just two examples of the biological wealth on offer in Thailand. Thailand has over 138 such wildlife sanctuaries and national parks, declared by the government. These unique places of natural beauty, rich in flora and fauna, are becoming popular destinations for eco-tourism. A number of these fascinating protected areas are successfully described and colourfully depicted in this interesting book by Stephen Elliott, a renowned biologist and naturalist working at Chiang Mai University and Gerald Cubitt, a remarkably gifted photographer. I would like to congratulate the authors for their extraordinary efforts in bringing together Thailand's beautiful natural resources in this concise, colourful and informative book, making it one of the best reference works concerned with biodiversity in Southeast Asia.

For readers who have never travelled to Thailand or those who wish to relive their visit, *The National Parks and Other Wild Places of Thailand* will provide both a wonderful introduction to and a stunning momento of Thailand's biological, historical, cultural and artistic treasures. I am certain that this book will prove extremely valuable in promoting the need to conserve biodiversity, create a greener environment and ultimately achieve a sustainable future for Thailand.

Visut Baimai
Director, The Biodiversity Research and Training Program
Mahidol University, Bangkok

INTRODUCTION

Thailand is a Kingdom of amazing biological diversity. From coral reefs and mangrove forests in the south, to misty mountains blanketed in lush forest in the north, this beautiful country has fascinated and intrigued both casual visitors and professional naturalists for more than a century. Spectacular scenery, some of the world's finest beaches and dive sites, impressive caves and waterfalls, as well as rich cultural diversity, make Thailand an ideal destination for eco-tourists.

Thailand lies between the Tropic of Cancer and the Equator, from 5° 37' to 20° 30' latitude north and from 97° 20' to 105° 39' longitude east. With a human population of more than 60 million and a rapidly developing economy, the country has lost much of its forest cover and wildlife in recent years. Thailand still, however, retains many of its natural treasures, and it is hoped that this book will inspire greater appreciation of them, as well as encourage increased efforts for their conservation.

With an area of 513,115 square kilometres (198,115 square miles), Thailand is divided into five main regions, each with some unique scenic and ecological features. The Central Region has some of Thailand's most extensive conservation areas and largest remaining populations of large herbivores and Tigers. Unique tropical forests and the best snorkelling sites in the Gulf of Thailand are the main features of the Southeast Region. Northern Thailand is best known for its striking montane scenery and hill-tribe cultures, whilst the Northeast (or Isaan) boasts Thailand's first national park and the most easily seen Asian Elephants in the country as well as the country's

most extensive pine forests and flower meadows. For marine attractions, the Southern Region (or Peninsular Thailand) is unsurpassed. Dramatic scenery, created by drowned limestone karst, sea caves, fine beaches and coral reefs in crystal-clear waters create one of the most varied environments in the Kingdom.

Thailand's Biological Wealth

On land, forests and their wildlife are the main ecological attractions. Thailand's forests are tremendously varied. In the south, the forest is similar to equatorial rainforest, with huge buttressed trees, rattan palms and a multitude of epiphytes and woody climbers, as well as Thailand's largest flower, the parasitic *Rafflesia kerrii*. In the northern mountains oaks, pines, and magnolias create a more temperate habitat for plants and animals usually associated with the Himalayas. In lowlands all over northern, eastern and western Thailand, seasonally dry deciduous forests predominate, such as deciduous dipterocarp forest, with an open canopy and grassy ground layer. These savannah-like forests once provided grazing for vast herds of Asian Elephants, deer and wild cattle, a sight now seen only in Thailand's larger conservation areas, such as the Western Forest Complex.

Thailand's vascular flora numbers approximately 15,000 species. The country is home to 285 mammal species (108 of which are bats), 962 bird species (10 per cent of the world total), 313 reptile species and 107 amphibian species. The number of insect species is estimated to be in excess of 70,000, including at least 1,200 butterfly species. Major initiatives are under way to quantify, classify and map Thailand's biodiversity, but it will be many years before the full extent of Thailand's biological richness is known.

A serene sunrise on the coast of Krabi Province (left). *This butterfly is one of at least 1,200 species known to occur in Thailand* (above).

Thailand's 2,600-kilometre (1,620-mile) coastline is equally fascinating and biologically diverse. Although coral reefs with multicoloured fish are the most attractive coastal feature, there are also breath-taking limestone cliffs towering over the ocean, pristine sandy beaches and mangrove swamps, which provide sanctuary to millions of migrating shorebirds.

Thailand's marine environment is divided between the Andaman Sea in the west and the Gulf of Thailand to the east. The islands of the Andaman Sea are among the most scenic in the world. Ko Surin and Tarutao, are where Thailand's most spectacular coral reefs have developed, providing habitat for more than 400 fish species and 200 species of hard coral and refuge for Whale Sharks, sea turtles, Manta Rays and the highly endangered Dugong. Although conditions in the Gulf of Thailand are not so ideal for coral growth, several marine parks provide diving opportunities, such as those at Ang Thong and Ko Chang.

Thailand's Protected Areas System

In order to protect this biological wealth, successive governments have built up an impressive system of protected areas. Since the early 1960s, 91 national parks and 47 wildlife sanctuaries, covering more than 15 per cent of the Kingdom, have been established. Numerous smaller conservation sites, such as non-hunting areas, forest parks, reserved forests, botanical gardens and biosphere reserves, provide additional protection to wildlife.

The Royal Forest Department manages these areas and is responsible for providing educational facilities, rehabilitating degraded sites, and preventing logging, hunting and fires. Each site has a headquarters, with a small staff of full-time officers, supported by larger numbers of part-time employees, who act as rangers and fire fighters.

National parks are created under the National Parks Act of 1961, to be 'preserved in their natural state for the benefit of public education and enjoyment'. Thailand's first national park, Khao Yai, was declared on 18 September 1962. At first, the national parks system grew fairly slowly. By 1972, only a further four parks had been declared (Phu Kradung, Thung Salaeng Luang, Khao Sam Roi Yot and Nam Nao); but, thereafter, the declaration of new national parks accelerated and still continues. Following a ban on commercial logging in reserved forests in 1989, 31 new parks were declared in the 1990s, absorbing many former logging concessions into the protected areas system. Today, national parks cover 45,889 square kilometres (28,680 square miles), 9 per cent of the country, conserving some of the most biologically rich forest areas in Southeast Asia.

Marine national parks are a more recent phenomenon. The Royal Forest Department declared Thailand's first marine national park, Khao Sam Roi Yot, in 1966, but it was not until 1993 that marine national parks were managed separately from the terrestrial parks. Marine parks were established to address growing concerns over Man's impact on marine ecosystems, including pollution, destruction of coral reefs, over-fishing and tourism development. Today, the Marine National Parks Division of the Royal Forest Department manages 18 sites totalling 5,216 square kilometres (2,013 square miles), of which 3,871 square kilometres (1,494 square miles) is ocean.

Wildlife sanctuaries are created under the Wild Animals Reservation and Protection Act of 1960. They are areas set aside for the 'conservation of wildlife habitat so that wildlife can freely breed and increase their populations in the natural environment'. Although fewer in number, wildlife sanctuaries tend to be larger than national parks.

Currently, 47 sanctuaries protect a total of 33,198 square kilometres (12,814 square miles), 6.5 per cent of the country, including some of the most significant forest habitats for wildlife in Southeast Asia. Unlike national parks, wildlife sanctuaries are not open to the general public, and tourism is strongly discouraged. Therefore, no wildlife sanctuaries are described in this book, except for Thung Yai Naresuan–Huay Kha Khaeng Wildlife Sanctuaries, which are included because of their World Heritage status.

Visiting Thailand's National Parks

Thailand has excellent roads and public transport, which make visiting national parks easy. For some parks, tour agencies in nearby towns and cities offer organized itineraries. For visitors who wish to plan their own trips, hired four-wheel-drive cars are the best way to get around, since attractions tend to be scattered over large distances. National park headquarters do not provide transport. Entrance fees are charged for most parks. Foreign visitors should expect to pay about five times more than Thai citizens.

Most national parks operate bungalows or dormitories to accommodate tourists, but these must be booked at least one month in advance by contacting the Royal Forest Department in Bangkok:

Accommodation Service,
National Park Division
The Royal Forest Department
Phaholyothin Road, Chatuchak
Bangkok
Thailand 10900

Tel. 02-579-7223, 02-579-5734

All national parks have campsites and some have tents for hire, but campsite facilities tend to be very basic. Privately operated resorts are also available on the periphery of many of the parks. Simple hotels or guesthouses can always be found in the nearest town.

Most national park headquarters operate simple restaurants, but park visitors should carry food and drink with them, especially when travelling away from main tourist attractions.

Other facilities include visitor information centres with small exhibitions, brochures and maps describing the main features of the park. Unfortunately for foreign visitors, most of this information is provided only in Thai. Walking trails vary from short, self-guided, nature trails with interpretative leaflets or signboards, to long treks of several days undertaken with park guides. Few park guides speak English, but English-speaking guides can sometimes be obtained through local tour agencies. However, there are several excellent English-language field guides that cover Thailand's flora and fauna (consult the section on further reading on page 172).

For most of the forested parks, light, long-sleeved shirts, long trousers, hiking boots and a hat are recommended for protection against insects, ticks and leeches. For mountainous parks, especially in the north, a pullover and jacket are essential, as well as a warm sleeping bag if staying overnight. Other essential equipment includes candles, a torch, a compass and a first-aid kit. Daily use of a sunscreen lotion is recommended.

Tourists are well catered for in Thailand's national parks with guided activities such as rafting on the Ping River (opposite, left), *campsites* (opposite, centre) *and information* (opposite, right). *Vast areas of forest* (below, left) *and sandy beaches* (below, right) *provide a wealth of scenic diversity and habitat.*

Mosquitoes and other insects transmit malaria and other diseases by day and night. Insect repellent should be applied during the daytime, and a mosquito net should be used at night. Before visiting parks, visitors should consult a doctor for the latest local information about malaria prophylaxis, vaccinations and other disease-prevention measures. Anyone developing a fever whilst visiting a national park should seek immediate medical advice. Several snakes in Thailand are venomous and their bites can be fatal, especially those of cobras, kraits, pit vipers and sea snakes. Snakebite victims should be kept calm and transported immediately to the nearest hospital.

Visitor Activities

The range of activities available in Thailand's national parks is almost as diverse as the wildlife that they contain. Opportunities to relax by waterfalls and on beaches or to follow short forest nature trails are provided in abundance. More adventurous visitors can try rock climbing or sea canoeing along the Krabi coast, diving around Ko Surin or rafting in the northern mountains. For those willing to carry a tent and supplies on their backs, there are numerous long distance hikes and helpful guides to lead the way. These provide the best opportunities to see large animals and the rarer species of birds.

Not all activities are tolerated in national parks, however. Visitors are reminded to camp only in designated areas, and not to start fires, which can destroy vast areas of forest. Obviously, hunting and collecting plants, insects or other biological specimens are strictly forbidden, and

Wild Water Buffaloes (below, left), *the Oriental Darter* (below, centre) *and Mucuna, a forest liana* (below, right) *are just a few examples of the wildlife that inhabits Thailand.*

there are fines for those who ignore the regulations. Garbage-collection in national parks is minimal, so visitors should carry all their rubbish out of the park when they depart.

Ecosystems in Danger

As in most tropical countries, Thailand's wild places are endangered. Deforestation is probably the most devastating problem. Since establishment of the first protected areas in the 1960s, Thailand's forest cover has been reduced from 53 per cent to about 22.8 per cent or 111,010 square kilometres (42,850 square miles). A ban on commercial logging in 1989 has helped to slow the destruction, but the deforestation rate still exceeds 1,000 square kilometres (386 square miles) per year (according to Royal Forest Department statistics), due to illegal logging, agricultural expansion and development projects.

Even where good forest survives, visitors are often surprised at the general scarcity of wildlife. This is due to uncontrolled hunting throughout the country. From young children with catapults to wealthy 'sport' hunters with rifles, the killing of wildlife is relentless. Hunters are occasionally apprehended in national parks by rangers, but the fines for hunting represent only a minor inconvenience compared with the value of wildlife products on the black market.

Habitat destruction and hunting have resulted in the extirpation of several species from the country. Schomburgk's Deer, endemic to the central plains of Thailand, became extinct in the 1930s. The Thai subspecies of the Brow-antlered Deer is now found only in zoos. The Kouprey and Javan Rhino have both disappeared from Thailand. Recent losses among the birds include Milky Stork, Giant Ibis and the endemic White-eyed River-martin.

The marine environment is endangered as well. Uncontrolled development of coastal resorts has increased marine pollution and disturbed the nesting beaches of sea turtles. A rise in sea temperatures, caused by global warming, has resulted in bleaching of corals in some areas. A walk along the high-tide lines of any of the islands of the Andaman Sea provides tragic testament to the vast quantities of garbage being dumped at sea. The highly endangered Dugong and giant Leatherback Sea Turtle are still slaughtered or die entangled in fishing nets.

Conservation in Thailand

Despite the seriousness of the problems, Thailand has made great strides in recent years to increase protection of wildlife. The creation of protected areas is vital for wildlife conservation, but they are of little value without effective management, based on sound scientific research. The Conservation Data Centre at Mahidol University's Department of Biology was one of the earliest attempts to map the distribution of Thailand's birds, mammals, reptiles and amphibians. Wildlife experts from all over the country fed information into a computer database that was used to refine the protected areas system and direct scarce conservation resources to where they might have greatest benefit. The Biodiversity Research and Training Programme, a Government initiative to prepare Thailand to ratify the Convention on Biodiversity, has helped to train a new generation of biologists to study and conserve the country's wildlife.

Wildlife-protection laws have recently been strengthened to bring Thailand in line with other member countries of the Convention on the International Trade in Endangered Species. More species than ever before are now protected by law, and Thailand's reputation as a conduit for trade in endangered species is diminishing. The Royal Forest Department operates several centres around the country to rescue confiscated wildlife but, so far, attempts to reintroduce species to natural habitats have been limited. A recent initiative by the World Wide Fund for Nature to reintroduce domestic Asia Elephants into their natural forest habitat in Northern Thailand is, however, having some success.

Protection of forests in national parks and a ban on commercial logging have failed to prevent continuing deforestation. The main challenge for conservationists today is to restore forests and wildlife where they have been destroyed. Government policy is to have 40 per cent of the country under forest and impressive projects have been initiaged to increase forest cover. A national project to restore 8,000 square kilometres (3,088 square miles) of forest, to mark the Golden Jubilee of His Majesty King Bhumibol Adulyadej, has increased participation by local people, government officers and private enterprise in practical conservation. The contribution to this project at Thap Lan National Park (see page 130) is a good example. In addition, research programmes, such as that implemented by the Forest Restoration Research Unit at Chiang Mai University, generate the vital scientific knowledge that gradually improves conservation efforts throughout the country. This project is developing new techniques to restore natural forest ecosystems on degraded sites for the conservation of biodiversity.

It is hoped that improved laws, better education and more scientific research will all contribute to a safer future for Thailand's national parks and other wild places.

On the forest floor skinks scurry through the leaf litter (below, left), *whilst pig-tailed Macaques roam in large troops* (below, right).

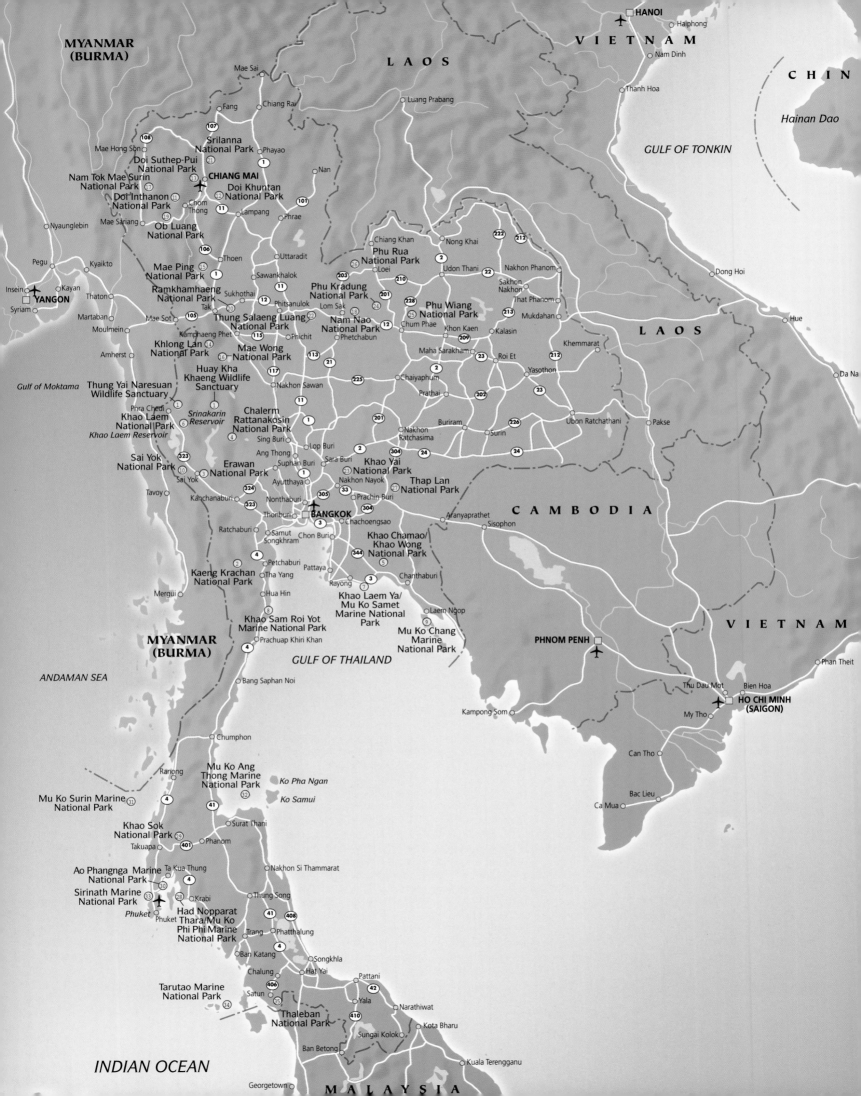

SOUTH CHINA SEA

KEY

──①──	Highway
──⟨201⟩──	Main Road
── · ── · ──	International boundary
Chiang Mai ○	City or major town
Takuapa ○	Village or small town
Srinakarin Reservoir	Water feature
✈	International airport

0	50	100	150	200	250	300 Kilometres

0	50	100	150 Miles

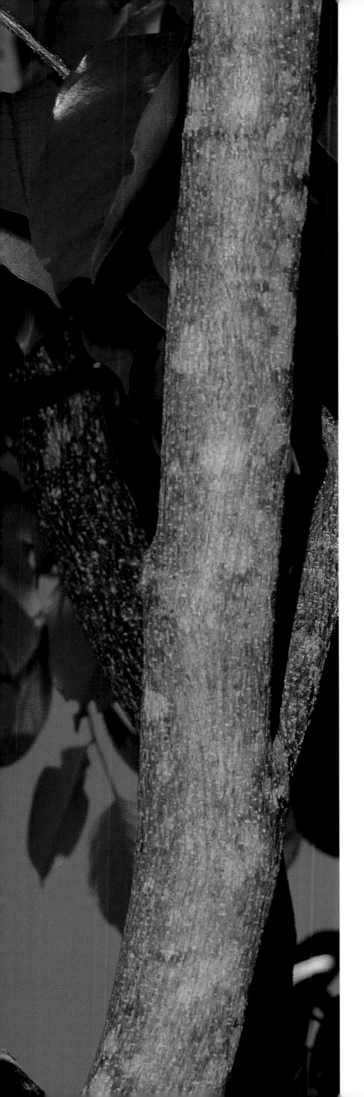

CENTRAL AND SOUTHEAST THAILAND

Central and southeast Thailand are the country's most heavily developed regions. Including the capital, Bangkok, the main rice-growing plains and largest industrial estates, it is perhaps surprising that Thailand's largest protected areas exist in the west of this region. The largest national park, Kaeng Krachan, is just three hours from Bangkok by car. Asian Elephants, deer, gibbons and hornbills are the main attractions.

Farther north, the Western Forest Complex is Southeast Asia's largest forest; with 14 contiguous protected areas (six wildlife sanctuaries and eight national parks), and an additional three parks proposed to complete the system. The complex will eventually cover 18,727 square kilometres (7,229 square miles). Co-ordinated conservation initiatives will provide Thailand's final opportunity to conserve viable populations of large mammals. The Western Forest Elephant Conservation Project, for example, protects 600 Asian Elephants.

Huay Kha Khaeng and Thung Yai Naresuan Wildlife Sanctuaries form the heart of the complex, a last stronghold for Wild Water Buffalo and the fabulous Green Peafowl. Nearby Erawan and Sai Yok National Parks have impressive caves and waterfalls, home to both the world's smallest and largest bat species. Khao Laem and Chalerm Rattanakosin National Parks help absorb animals dispersing from core areas of the complex.

There are three marine national parks in the Gulf of Thailand. Khao Sam Roi Yot has important coastal marshes and is a refuge for migrating shorebirds; Ko Samet has suffered greatly from tourism, but tranquil beaches can still be found; and Ko Chang preserves some of the Gulf's finest coral reefs.

THUNG YAI NARESUAN–HUAY KHA KHAENG

Wildlife Sanctuaries and World Heritage Site

The combined wildlife sanctuaries of Thung Yai Naresuan and Huay Kha Khaeng comprise Thailand's most impressive conservation area and, indeed, the largest in mainland Southeast Asia. With a combined area of 6,427 square kilometres (2,481 square miles), these wildlife sanctuaries constitute the core of the Western Forest Complex, a vast collection of interconnected conservation sites that protect the best habitat for large herbivores, and their predators, and the most diverse range of birds, insects, reptiles and amphibians in the country.

Opposite, above: *Dense deciduous dipterocarp forests make Huay Kha Khaeng one of the last strongholds for many of Thailand's largest mammals.*

Opposite, below left: *The elusive Clouded Leopard is one of seven cat species confirmed for Huay Kha Khaeng.*

Opposite, below right: *The main river through Huay Kha Khaeng is a vital habitat for the Wild Water Buffalo.*

Above, right: *The Grey Peacock-pheasant forages for fruits and insects on the ground in evergreen forest.*

Previous pages:
Page 18: *The Garden Fence Lizard can change colour rapidly, depending on its mood.* Page 19: *The Central Plains constitute Thailand's most important rice-growing area.*

Established between 1974 and 1991 and with an area of 3,647 square kilometres (1,408 square miles), Thung Yai Naresuan is the largest single conservation site in Thailand. It is named after King Naresuan The Great who regained Siam's independence from Burma in the 16th century. Ranging in elevation from 100 to 1,811 metres above sea level (328 to 5,942 feet), it has recently been divided into two administrative units (an eastern one and a western one) for easier management. 'Thung Yai' means a large field, referring to vast open grasslands studded with cycads and trees on rolling hills at the centre of the wildlife sanctuary. These grasslands provide essential grazing for large ungulates and are maintained by frequent fires.

Huay Kha Khaeng is smaller at 2,780 square kilometres (1,073 square miles), and was established between 1972 and 1992. The sanctuary is hilly, ranging in elevation from 200 to 1,554 metres above sea level (656 to 5,068 feet) and, without the presence of villages within its boundaries, it is in a more pristine condition than Thung Yai.

A Diversity of Wildlife

Both sanctuaries contain a diverse range of forests, from deciduous dipterocarp forest in the lowlands to mixed deciduous forests at mid elevations and evergreen

Location: Northwest of Bangkok, in the provinces of Kanchanaburi, Uthai Thani and Tak, extending west to the border with Myanmar.

Climate: Monsoonal, mean annual rainfall 1,700 mm (67 in) or more; rainy season May–October; cool season November–January (minimum temperature 8°C/46°F); hot dry season February–April (maximum temperature 37°C/99°F).

When to Go: Cool season best for forest treks and highest diversity of birds; early wet season probably best for large herbivores.

Access: Access points to Huay Kha Khaeng reached travelling west from Uthai Thani and following Highway 3011 and turnoffs to Ban Rai and Ban Tai, or Highway 3282 to Lan Sak. Thung Yai via roads north from Kanchanburi–Sangkhla Buri Highway (323) near the Khao Laem Dam. Four-wheel-drive cars essential. No public transport.

Permits: Wildlife sanctuaries are not open to the public, permits from the Royal Forest Department in Bangkok or the Chiefs of the Wildlife Sanctuary Headquarters.

Equipment: Camping equipment, protection against mosquitoes and leeches, light clothes and strong shoes; warm clothing for the cool season.

Facilities: Tourist facilities are not provided in wildlife sanctuaries.

Watching Wildlife: Large herbivores, primates, large cats, high diversity of birds, Green Peafowl, Red-headed Vultures.

Visitor Activities: Forest walks, wildlife photography, birdwatching.

Right: Tigers still survive in Thung Yai–Huay Kha Khaeng. Roaming over vast areas to find their prey, these top predators require huge protected areas to maintain viable populations.

Below: Along the many rivers that criss-cross these wildlife sanctuaries, a great diversity of drag-onflies and damselflies can be seen. Males stake out territories to attract females by perching on grass or twigs.

forests on the mountains and along the many streams and rivers that flow through the sanctuaries. This wide range of habitats provides a refuge for Thailand's most diverse wildlife community. Although species lists for these sanctuaries are far from complete, Mahidol University's Conservation Data Centre lists 355 confirmed bird species, 85 mammals (including 14 bats), 45 reptiles and 23 frogs or toads for Huay Kha Khaeng. Confirmed species for Thung Yai Naresuan include 338 birds, 60 mammals (five bats), 27 reptiles and 13 frogs or toads.

Tigers and Other Predators

Thung Yai–Huay Kha Khaeng probably support more Tigers than any other protected area in Thailand. Once widespread throughout the country, Tigers have been reduced to probably no more than 250 individuals, in tiny scattered populations. The Western Forest Complex is perhaps the last hope for survival of this species in Thailand. Even there, however, sightings of Tigers are rare, but visitors might be lucky enough to spot their footprints or hear their roars at night. In addition to Tigers, these wildlife sanctuaries provide a refuge to several other cats including Fishing Cat, Leopard Cat, Jungle Cat, Golden Cat, Clouded Leopard and Leopard.

Left: *Although it resembles the docile domestic buffalo, the Wild Water Buffalo is much larger, faster moving and more aggressive.*

Below: Plumbago indica *is a rare scrambling herb with medicinal properties.*

Perhaps even more dangerous to herbivores than the solitary cats is the Asian Wild Dog, which hunts in packs of up to 20 individuals. Mostly feeding on deer and Common Wild Pigs, these carnivores occasionally attack the young of Banteng or Gaur. Another canid, the Asiatic Jackal, also occurs in the wildlife sanctuaries, often feeding on carrion left by Tigers.

Large Herbivores

Large cats could not survive without an abundance of prey species and Thung Yai–Huay Kha Khaeng abounds with large herbivores.

Three out of Thailand's four species of wild cattle live in Thung Yai–Huay Kha Khaeng. The rarest of these is the Wild Water Buffalo. The 40–60 individuals that live along the rivers of the southern part of Huay Kha Khaeng may be Asia's last truly wild population of this species. Larger than the Domestic Water Buffalo, this group represents a genetic resource of incalculable value to agriculture in Asia, where buffaloes are the most impor-tant draft animals. Banteng, a close relative of domestic cows in Asia, and Gaur, a massive black forest ox, are the other two wild cattle species in the wildlife sanctuaries. Thailand's fourth wild cattle species, the Kouprey, is now probably extirpated from the country, but might still survive in Laos and Cambodia.

Asian Elephants occur in small, scattered herds throughout the area and other endangered species of large herbivore, such as Malayan Tapir and Fea's Muntjak, can also be found there.

Birds

Thung Yai–Huay Kha Khaeng is a paradise for bird-watchers. These wildlife sanctuaries are the last strong-holds of several rare bird species. Dependent upon riverine habitat are the highly endangered White-winged Duck and the magnificent Green Peafowl, the world's largest pheasant species. In the breeding season, male Green Peafowl attract females to open areas near streams with their trumpeting calls and fantastic displays of shimmering green tail feathers. The last resident population of perhaps a dozen Red-headed Vultures cling to existence in Thung Yai–Huay Kha Khaeng, the last remaining place in Thailand with enough carcasses of wild animals for them to feed on. Other notable rare birds include Kalij Pheasant, Grey Peacock Pheasant and Rufous-necked Hornbill.

The Rise of a Conservation Movement

In the 1980s, a famous environmental conflict in Thung Yai Naresuan triggered the growth of a powerful conservation movement in Thailand. The Electricity Generating Authority of Thailand proposed building the 187-metre (614-foot) high Nam Choan Hydroelectric Dam on a tributary of the Khwae Yai River. The reservoir formed would have divided the wildlife sanctuary into three separate

Above: *A magnificent male Green Peafowl displays by fanning out its tail feathers to attract a female. Perhaps 300– 400 individuals survive along the lowland rivers of Huay Kha Khaeng.*

Right: *Riverine habitats provide a vital refuge for a huge diversity of animals in the dry season. Birds, mammals, insects, reptiles and amphibians all become concentrated in these areas when drought and fire threatens them.*

fragments, destroying critical riverine habitat of the Green Peafowl and disrupting annual migration routes of Asian Elephants, deer and wild cattle. For the first time in Thailand's history, more than 40 disparate environmental groups united to oppose the dam, with protest rallies and petitions. They were successful, and on

4 April 1988, the Government shelved the project. This was the first time that conservation groups had successfully opposed a major Government initiative. They had put environmental concerns firmly on Thailand's political agenda and paved the way for Thung Yai–Huay Kha Khaeng to be declared a UNESCO World Heritage Site in December 1991. Bolstered by their success, environmentalists also prevented the Thai Plywood Company from opening a logging concession in Huay Kha Khaeng a few years later.

Above: *An adult Gaur and calf. This massive species of wild cattle grazes on the fresh grass sprouting under the open canopy of deciduous forest early in the rainy season. Unfortunately, they are still shot for trophies.*

Heritage in Danger

Despite being saved from the dam and logging, however, this World Heritage Site is still in danger. Asian Elephants, wild cattle and large cats are the main targets of illegal trophy hunters and traders in wildlife products. Constant vigilance is necessary to solve this problem, but rangers are poorly paid and lack the motivation required to take on poachers armed with AK47 rifles, when they have only shot guns. Another serious threat to the wildlife sanctuaries is forest fire, which ravages large areas every dry season. In Thung Yai, the presence of villages within the wildlife sanctuary and an expanding mining industry also threaten forests and wildlife.

Left: *Forest rangers on patrol to protect the natural heritage of Thailand's largest conservation area. Despite their efforts, hunters and fire pose a continuous threat to the wildlife.*

KAENG KRACHAN NATIONAL PARK

Thailand's Largest Park

Philip D. Round, one of Thailand's most eminent ornithologists, described Kaeng Krachan as 'the brightest jewel in the diadem of Thailand's National Parks'. He was not exaggerating. Not only does the park boast a bird fauna of at least 355 species, but it also retains thriving populations of large mammal species that have been severely reduced elsewhere. Among its 58 confirmed mammal species are Asian Elephant, Asiatic Black Bear, Malayan Sun Bear, Serow, Lesser Mouse Deer, Feae's Muntjak, Wild Dog, Asiatic Jackal, Malayan Tapir, Binturong, Malay Pangolin, Clouded Leopard and Tiger. The reason for the remarkably rich fauna of Kaeng Krachan is its vast

area of dense forest, including evergreen forest, mixed evergreen deciduous forest and deciduous dipterocarp forest, lying adjacent to a similarly large forested area in Myanmar. An extensive system of tracks and footpaths makes this park ideal for long-distance nature treks.

Established in 1981, Kaeng Krachan is Thailand's largest park, with an area of 2,915 square kilometres (1,125 square miles), of which an estimated 95 per cent is still forested. Situated just a three-hour drive southwest of Bangkok, it is also one of the most accessible places to see large mammals.

The park is formed of rolling, forested hills, gradually rising westwards into mountains, reaching a maximum elevation of 1,207 metres (3,960 feet) at the summit of Khao Panoenthong. The western boundary of the park follows the international border with Myanmar.

Kaeng Krachan Reservoir

The park has been well protected because it is a vital water catchment area for the Kaeng Krachan Reservoir, created when Thailand's largest earth dam was constructed to provide electricity and irrigation water for agriculture. The area of the reservoir is 45.5 square kilometres (17½ square miles) and it includes up to 30 islands, depending on the water level. Many visitors

Opposite, top: The multi-layered forest canopy provides habitat for a wide range of primates and a host of birds.

Opposite, below left: The black fruits of the Pioneer treelet, Clerodendrum glandulosum, are edible by birds. They contain a powerful emetic used in traditional medicine.

Opposite, below right: The largest member of the civet family in Thailand, the Binturong is equipped with a long prehensile tail, which helps it balance in the tree tops.

Above, right: A juvenile Grey-headed Fish-eagle is one of many endangered bird species that can be seen.

Location: Phetchaburi and Prachuap Khiri Khan Provinces, southwest from Bangkok.

Climate: Annual rainfall 1,040 mm (41 in), 90 per cent June–November. Mean annual temperature 28°C (82°F), cooler December–January (25°C/77°F), hotter March–July.

When to Go: November–February provides the best road conditions and migrant birds. Avoid public holidays.

Access: Four-wheel-drive vehicle essential (motorbikes and cycles not allowed). From Bangkok, follow Highway 4 to Phetchaburi; proceed to Thayang, turn right onto Highway 3187 and then 3499. Follow signs to Kaeng Krachan Dam. Park headquarters 4 kilometres (2 miles) beyond the dam.

Permits: The park operates a bewildering system of permits, purchased at the park headquarters, during office hours. Entry to the Panoenthong track is allowed only during 5 a.m.–10 a.m. and 2.30 p.m.–3 p.m. and exits only during 12 noon–1 p.m. and 4.30 p.m.–6 p.m. For information, telephone 032-459-291.

Equipment: Light clothes and boots (warmer clothes if climbing Khao Panoenthong), insect repellent, full camping equipment and malaria/leech protection.

Facilities: Camping at Bankrang, Panoenthong, Tortip and park headquarters, where bungalows are for rent; restaurant, visitor centre, leaflets and maps and guides for hire. Boats for charter.

Watching Wildlife: Large ungulates, primates and large cats. Very diverse forest and water birds.

Visitor Activities: Long distance treks and camping, boat trips, visiting caves and waterfalls.

Map labels:
THAILAND
Bangkok
Kaeng Krachan National Park
Kaeng Krachan Reservoir
Phetchaburi River
To Tha Yang
Khao Panoenthong
1207m (3960ft)
Hua Chang Cave
Bankrang Camp
Park Headquarters
Sam Yoi
MYANMAR (BURMA)
THAILAND
N

Above: Kaeng Krachan is one of the few parks in Thailand large enough to sustain a small population of Tigers. These powerful predators favour dense forest, where they prey on mammals up to the size of Sambar and Banteng.

Right: Wild bees' nests can be found hanging from the branches of trees.

come to Kaeng Krachan simply to relax on the shore of the reservoir, near the park headquarters, and enjoy camping, swimming and boat trips. Birds around the reservoir and its tributaries include Little Grebe, Chinese Pond Heron, Osprey, White-breasted Waterhen and up to ten different species of kingfisher. Along stream edges, Thailand's largest frog species, the Malayan Giant Frog, can be seen. However, the park's most impressive wildlife attractions lie 30 kilometres (18½ miles) west of the headquarters, where dense forest begins.

Exploring the Forest

A single-lane track to Panoenthong Camp, suitable for four-wheel-drive vehicles, a network of walking trails and several campsites enable visitors to penetrate deep into the forest, but tickets must be purchased at the park headquarters before beginning the journey.

Large evergreen trees dominate the forest canopy, including *Tetrameles nudiflora*, *Acrocarpus fraxinifolius*, *Elaeocarpus grandiflorus*, *Stereospermum fimbriatum*, *Barringtonia macrostachya* and *Crateva magna*.

Asian Elephants, Banteng and Leopards are often seen along the road at night. The Indochinese Leopards

of Kaeng Krachan have been studied by radio tracking. Lon Grassman, a researcher at Kasetsart University, showed that they range over 8.8-18.0 square kilometres (3 to 7 square miles) and eat mainly Hog Badger, Barking Deer and Common Wild Pig, all of which are abundant in the area and likely to be seen at night.

One of the easiest ways to view wildlife is to camp at Bankrang, 15 kilometres (24 miles) along the Panoenthong track from the entry checkpoint, and walk quietly along the main track and footpaths at dawn or

Above, left: *Sun Bears are equally at home on the ground or in trees, where they feed on bees' nests and fruit, and construct nests from small branches.*

Above, right: *Asian Elephants are sometimes seen at night along the road to Panoenthong Camp, but the visitor is more likely to come across tracks or droppings than the animal itself.*

Right: *A Drynaria rigidula fern grows on a large evergreen forest tree that dominates the forest canopy. This epiphytic plant grows on tree trunks and branches and absorbs nutrients from rainfall and detritus trapped by its fronds.*

Right: The Blue-winged Pitta is a common breeding visitor at Kaeng Krachan during the rainy season.

Far right: This epiphytic orchid (Rhynchostylis coelestis) has found a precarious root-hold on the trunk of a tree. Such orchids do not penetrate their 'hosts', but use their support to gain a place in the sun.

Below: The Indochinese Leopards of Kaeng Krachan have been the subject of intensive scientific study that has provided detailed information on their behaviour and dietary habits.

dusk. In the morning, White-handed Gibbons rouse campers with their penetrating songs, whilst crashes in the forest canopy betray the presence of Banded Leaf-monkey, Dusky Langur and macaques (Pig-tailed, Stump-tailed and Long-tailed). From Bankrang, forest rangers guide visitors to Hua Chang Cave, aptly named after one of its limestone formations, which strongly resembles the head of an elephant.

Parasitic Plants

Botanists will be interested in several rare parasitic plants that grow nearby, such as *Sapria himalayana*, in the same family as the world's largest flower, *Rafflesia*. Feeding on the roots of lianas, this curious plant develops buds the size of baseballs or cricket balls, which push through the leaf litter and open into bright red flowers shaped like 10-pointed stars, covered with white spots. The flowers smell like putrid meat to attract the carrion flies that pollinate them. Several *Balanophora* species, which parasitize tree roots and look more like fungi than flowering plants, are also common in the area.

Birdwatcher's Paradise

Birdwatchers may spot up to six species of hornbill, eight barbets, 15 woodpeckers, seven broadbills and five pittas.

Some of the rarer bird species include Grey-headed Fish-eagle, Blue-rumped Parrot, White-fronted Scops-owl, Barred Eagle-owl, Plain-pouched Hornbill, Olive-backed Woodpecker, Brown-chested Flycatcher and Ratchet-tailed Treepie. The latter is a recent new record for Thailand, previously known only from northern Vietnam, Laos and southern China. The park is also one of the last refuges for the endangered Woolly-necked Stork.

Long-distance Nature Adventures

For hardy adventurers an overnight trek to the highest point in the park (the summit of Khao Panoenthong) provides a good chance of sighting Asian Elephant, Gaur, Banteng and Sambar Deer. The ascent starts from the Panoenthong campsite at 'Km 30' on the main track. It takes at least six hours to complete the 10-kilometre (6-mile) climb. At the summit, campers rising early in the morning are rewarded with spectacular views of forested valleys blanketed in clouds, which slowly evaporate as the sun warms the atmosphere. From Khao Panoenthong summit treks of several days can be undertaken to Tortip Waterfall, a cataract with 18 steps, and along the Phetchaburi River, passing hot springs along the way. Guides from the park headquarters are essential for all these treks.

ERAWAN NATIONAL PARK

Thailand's Most Beautiful Waterfalls

Erawan is Thailand's most popular national park. Record numbers of visitors are attracted to the famous waterfalls near the park headquarters, considered by many to be the most beautiful in Thailand, where visiting waterfalls is one of the most popular recreational pastimes.

Inevitably, the area around the waterfalls suffers from overcrowding and tourism development, but the park also has more remote areas with dense forest that provides habitat for at least 314 bird species and 103 mammal species, and many caves that are hardly visited at all. Created in 1975, the park covers 550 square kilometres (212 square miles) of the Tenasserim Hills. It consists of a rolling plateau of granite and limestone hills, reaching a maximum elevation of

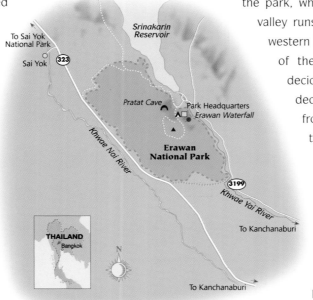

Opposite, above: *Beautiful cascades like this one have made Erawan Thailand's most popular national park.*

Opposite, below left: *The Spot-billed Pelican is an endangered species in Thailand and an exceedingly scarce visitor to Erawan National Park.*

Opposite, below right: *Pratat Cave, with its stalagmites and stalactites, is one of many caves in Erawan National Park.*

Above, right: *The Painted Jezebel is a rare butterfly, usually living high in the canopy of evergreen forest.*

996 metres (3,268 feet), sandwiched between two river valleys. The Khwae Yai River and the Srinakarin Reservoir form the northern and eastern boundary of the park, whilst the Khwae Noi River valley runs along the southern and western boundary. The vegetation of the park is mostly mixed deciduous forest and bamboo deciduous forest, recovering from extensive logging in the past.

The Waterfalls

Both the park and the waterfalls are named after the mount of the god, Indra, an elephant with three heads, and a powerful symbol in Thai culture. A limestone formation at the uppermost of the falls causes water to emerge in three spouts during the rainy season, said to resemble Erawan's three trunks. The entire waterfall system consists of seven tiers, dropping a total of 1,500 metres (4,921 feet). Although none of the falls are particularly large, they are very attractive in the dappled sunlight that penetrates the forest canopy. Water glides over limestone formations into azure-blue pools, teeming with Greater Brook Carp and other fish. Swimming is allowed in some of the pools. Concrete steps and handrails provide easy access to the falls, but detract from their natural beauty. The upper tiers are quieter and more natural. Several self-guided, circular nature trails enable visitors to ascend the falls and return to the headquarters via a different route, following paths through dense bamboo deciduous forest.

Location: Kanchanaburi Province, approximately 60 km (37 miles) northwest of the provincial capital.

Climate: Situated in the rain shadow of the Tenasserim Hills, the area has a mean annual rainfall of less than 1,500 mm (59 in); rainy season May–October; cool season November–February (mean minimum temperature 21°C/70°F); hot, dry season January–April (temperatures often exceed 40°C/104°F).

When to Go: It is wise to avoid the severe overcrowding at weekends and public holidays.

Access: From Kanchanaburi City, follow Highway 3199. Pass through the checkpoint for the Srinakarin Dam, then turn left and follow the signs. A public bus service runs twice a day between Kanchanaburi and the park headquarters.

Permits: An entrance fee is charged.

Equipment: Light clothing and tough footwear for forest walks; a torch for caves.

Facilities: At the park headquarters, bungalows for rent and camping; a visitor centre with exhibition and brochures; a huge carpark and many restaurants.

Watching Wildlife: Serow, deer, wild pigs, squirrels, civets and bats. High diversity of birds: kingfishers, hornbills, raptors and the rare Limestone Wren-babbler.

Visitor Activities: Forest walks; birdwatching; visiting caves and waterfalls; swimming.

Right: *Pit vipers have a large temperature-sensitive pit between the nostril and the eye used to sense their prey. The Pope's Pit-Viper lurks in shrubs and undergrowth in evergreen forest. Its bite is highly venomous.*

Below: *The Northern Forest Crested Lizard searches for insects, mostly on tree trunks and on the forest floor in deciduous forest.*

Prehistoric Caves

Limestone areas of the park are riddled with caves. At least six cave systems are open to the public. Not only are these caves adorned with impressive formations, including beautiful stalactites and stalagmites, but some also contain evidence of Thailand's earliest human inhabitants. At Ta Duang Cave there are rock paintings of trees and human figures of unknown age. One scene shows men carrying what might be a large circular drum. Prehistoric inhabitants also left behind pottery and hand tools. Rua Cave (or boat cave) lacks stalagmites or stalactites, but contains several boat-shaped coffins carved from whole tree trunks. Human facial features are carved into the upper parts of the coffins. The date of these relics is unknown. Show respect when visiting these caves, as local people believe spells and guardian spirits protect them.

Birdwatching

The park supports a remarkably diverse bird community, characteristic of the bamboo deciduous forest and mixed deciduous forest. Some of the rarer species include Mountain Hawk Eagle, Yellow-footed Pigeon, Alexandrine Parakeet, Brown-chested Flycatcher, Japanese Paradise-flycatcher and Spot-winged Starling.

Five species of hornbill have been recorded in the park, including the endangered Plain-pouched Hornbill.

Along the streams and around the reservoirs many kingfishers can be seen, including Common, Blue-eared, Banded and Ruddy. The Limestone Wren-babbler is a speciality, restricted to limestone areas.

Mammals

Mammals are not particularly common or easy to see, but the park does support at least 40 species of bat, including Kitti's Hog-nosed Bat, the world's smallest. Some of the rarer mammal species that have been recorded in the park include Asiatic Jackal, Banded Linsang, Banded Palm-civet, Fishing Cat, Jungle Cat, Golden Cat, Clouded Leopard, Leopard, Tiger, Malay Tapir, Feae's Muntjak Deer and Banteng, but all are exceedingly scarce and rarely seen. More easily observed are Common Wild Pig, Common Barking Deer and, in steep limestone areas, Serow. A few Asian Elephants occasionally migrate into the park from surrounding protected areas.

Walkers in the forest should beware of venomous snakes, which are common in the area, including Banded Krait and King Cobra. A total of 43 reptile species have been recorded in the park.

Above: *The Banded Palm-civet is considered to be vulnerable to extinction. It is a scarce mammal in Erawan, searching the forest floor at night for insects, fruit and small mammals.*

Left: *Aquamarine pools teeming with carp are an attractive feature of waterfalls in limestone landscapes.*

CHALERM RATTANAKOSIN NATIONAL PARK

Caves and Waterfalls

Established in February 1980, this tiny 59-square-kilometre (23-square-mile) park is one of the smallest in the country. Yet packed within its confined borders are historical sites that mark turning-points in Thai history, spectacular caves and sink holes, beautiful waterfalls and serene forest trails. One of the lesser-known national parks in Kanchanaburi Province, Chalerm Rattanakosin provides a quieter alternative to the more popular and overcrowded parks nearby, such as Erawan and Sai Yok.

The park consists of limestone mountains, forming part of the Tenasserim Hills, reaching a maximum elevation of 1,257 metres (4,124 feet) at Khao Kamphaeng. The area is

included in the Western Forest Complex, along with 13 other protected areas; an attempt at co-ordinated management of the largest remaining forest area in Southeast Asia. It adjoins the biologically richer Salak Pra Wildlife Sanctuary to the south and is slightly separated from Srinakarin National Park to the north.

Most of the park is covered in fairly intact mixed deciduous forest, although bamboo is common in some parts, indicating past logging. Evergreen forest occurs in smaller areas along stream valleys and at higher elevations.

Wildlife

The park has not been extensively surveyed for wildlife. At least 70 bird species have been recorded, but this relatively low number probably reflects lack of research rather than low diversity. For other groups, numbers of species are unknown.

Common resident birds include Spotted Dove, Vernal Hanging Parrot, Green-billed Malkoha, Blue-throated and Blue-eared Barbets, Hainan Blue Flycatcher, Black-naped Monarch and Olive-backed Sunbird, whilst those more rarely seen include Orange-breasted Trogon, Great Hornbill and Limestone Wren-babbler. Red-throated Flycatcher is a common winter visitor.

Large mammals are scarce and difficult to see in Chalerm Rattanakosin. White-handed Gibbons are still

Opposite, above: This common ground fern, Dryopteris ludens, *soaks up the sun through a gap in the forest canopy.*

Opposite, below left: Roundleaf Bats are one of the more common groups of cave-roosting bats found in Thailand.

Opposite, below right: The roots of a strangling fig wrapped around a tree. Figs do not 'strangle' trees, but kill them by competing for light, nutrients and water.

Above, right: Fungi are important to all forest ecosystems, breaking down dead wood and recycling nutrients.

Location: Kanchanaburi province, 97 km (60 miles) northwest of the provincial capital.

Climate: Mean annual rainfall 1,146 mm (45 in), mean annual temperature 28°C (82°F); rainy season May–October; cool season November–January (minimum temperature 17°C/63°F); hot, dry season February–April (maximum temperature 38°C/100°F).

When to Go: The cool season is most comfortable for forest walks.

Access: From Kanchanaburi City, follow Highway 323, then 3086 north to Ban Nong Prue. Just before Ban Nong Prue, turn west on the road signposted Than Lod, 22 km (14 miles) to the park headquarters. Public buses between Kanchanaburi and Dan Chang stop at Ban Nong Prue, from where local transport can be hired to the park headquarters.

Permits: None required; entrance fees charged for the caves.

Equipment: Light clothing and boots for forest walks; a torch for caves; swimming gear; a mosquito net and insect repellent are advisable if camping.

Facilities: Bungalows for rent and camping facilities, restaurants and shops around the park headquarters; a visitor centre with a small exhibition; guides available for forest treks.

Watching Wildlife: Birds, small mammals and gibbons.

Visitor Activities: Forest walks; birdwatching; visiting caves and waterfalls.

Above: *Although butterflies and moths abound at Chalerm Rattanakosin, no comprehensive survey has been carried out. This butterfly species is Thauria alicis.*

Above, right: *As the name suggests, the Limestone Wren-babbler is a speciality of limestone karst areas. It is usually seen in small groups foraging amongst fragmented rocks, where it also constructs its domed nest.*

relatively common, and their early morning choruses can be heard in the more remote western parts of the park. A few Asian Elephants may occasionally migrate into southern parts of the park from Salak Pra Wildlife Sanctuary. Although occasional reports of tracks and signs of large cats and bears persist, they probably disappeared from the park in the 1970s. The largest mammals likely still to be present in the park are Lesser Mouse Deer, Serow, Common Barking Deer, Common Wild Pig and several species of squirrel and civet. Caves in the remoter areas of the park shelter several bat species.

Waterfalls, Caves and Forest Trails

The main tourist attractions of the park are two caves. Tum Than Lod Noi, situated close to the park headquarters, is a 300-metre-long open-ended cave with a subterranean stream flowing through it. A well-worn trail leads from this cave past Trai Trung Waterfalls to another larger cave. Tum Than Lod Yai is an impressive sinkhole, open to the sky, with a sweeping natural stone archway that traverses the river. The path leads under the arch to a tranquil Buddhist meditation centre. The nature trail provides an informative introduction to evergreen forest. The forest is well-preserved with some massive *Hopea* and *Dipterocarpus* trees.

Historical Significance

Originally the park was named Tum Than Lod, after its famous caves, but in 1982 it was renamed Chalerm Rattanakosin to mark the bicentenary of the Chakri dynasty and declaration of Bangkok as the nation's capital. The Chakri dynasty, the current royal family of Thailand, was founded in 1782, when General Chao Phaya Chakri moved the country's capital city from Thonburi across the Chao Phraya River, to its current location. He ruled from 1782 until 1809AD. Before becoming King, the general fought against invading Burmese armies as they marched through what has become Chalerm Rattanakosin National Park, en route to destroy Thailand's former capital, Ayutthaya. Within the national park archaeologists have unearthed spears, charms believed to protect warriors from harm during battle, and human remains dating from that period, as well as prehistoric relics from the Stone Age.

Kings of the Chakri dynasty are known as Rama (Rama I, Rama II, and so on). They have reigned over Thailand until this day. The current King, Bhumibol Adulyadej, is Rama IX. The word 'rattanakosin' is part of Bangkok's very lengthy official name. Rattanakosin is the district of Bangkok that includes the Grand Palace and Sanam Luang.

KHAO CHAMAO–KHAO WONG NATIONAL PARK

Twin Mountains and Intoxicating Fish

Created in 1975, this national park is divided into two separate parts that protect two very different mountain peaks in Chantaburi and Rayong Provinces. The larger portion of the park is centred around the higher of the two mountains, the granite massif of Khao Chamao (1,028 metres/ 3,373 feet elevation), which retains the last substantial forest in Rayong Province, as well as small populations of large mammals and some very popular waterfalls. In contrast, Khao Wong is a limestone peak with some spectacular caves. The park is the origin of the Prasae River and provides vital irrigation water to fertile orchards of durian and other fruit trees in these rich agricultural provinces.

Intoxicating Fish

The name Khao Chamao means 'Drunken Mountain' on account of the Soro Brook Carp that live in pools below the waterfalls near the park headquarters. According to folklore the carp consume large quantities of fruits, known locally as *look gabow*, which contain toxins and are a traditional treatment for leprosy. The carp are unaffected by these toxins, but concentrate them in their flesh. Anyone eating the fish, however, becomes

Above, right: *This park retains a small but growing population of Asian Elephants. They sometimes raid fruit orchards near the park boundary.*

inebriated, disoriented or worse. Spared from the attention of local fishermen, the carp have become abundant, especially in Wang Matcha, a short distance along the waterfall trail from the park headquarters. There, whenever food is thrown into the water, the pool is transformed into a writhing mass of black-and-gold fish, some more than 50 centimetres (20 inches) long. The Soro Brook Carp is found in mountain streams from India to Thailand, and feeds on fruits, leaves and insects.

Large Mammals

Despite the park's small size (83 square kilometres/ 32 square miles), the evergreen and mixed deciduous forests that blanket Khao Chamao–Khao Wong retain small populations of several large mammals. Thanks to a recent reduction in hunting, both the Banteng and Asian Elephant populations may actually be increasing. In the 1980s Asian Elephants probably numbered less than 15 individuals. Today park rangers estimate their population at approximately 30. Unfortunately some elephants have begun to damage fruit orchards outside the park, causing conflict with local people. Recently, villagers retaliated by poisoning a female elephant and her baby. The preserved baby is on display in the visitor centre.

The park is one of the most important protected areas in the country for Pileated Gibbon. Common Wild

Location: Midway between, and 70 km (44 miles) from, provincial capitals of Rayong and Chantaburi, southeast from Bangkok.

Climate: Annual rainfall averages over 3,000 mm (118 in), more than 90 per cent falling May–October; driest November–March; mean annual temperature 26°C (79°F), coolest November–February, hottest April and June.

When to Go: Any time of the year, but avoid public holidays.

Access: By car, follow Highway 3 east from Rayong. 7 km (4½ miles) east of Klaeng at Ban Khao Din, turn north on Highway 3377 for 16 km (10 miles) to Ban Nam Sai. There, turn east along a narrow road, following signs to the park headquarters.

Permits: An entrance fee is charged. Access to the waterfalls allowed only from 6 a.m. to 6 p.m.

Equipment: For walking in the forest, light clothes, strong boots and insect repellent; for visiting caves, a torch.

Facilities: At the park headquarters, information centre with small exhibition, maps and information leaflets, well-organized system of trails with guides available; restaurants, small shops and a huge carpark. Six bungalows, (six to eight people each) can be booked by contacting the Forest Department in Bangkok. Campsites at the park headquarters and Klong Pla Kang.

Watching Wildlife: Asian Elephant, Banteng, Pileated Gibbon. Soro Brook Carp, in pools beneath the waterfalls, are a speciality of this park.

Visitor Activities: Visiting waterfalls, caving, birdwatching and guided nature trails.

Pig, Sambar Deer, Barking Deer and Long-tailed Macaques are fairly common in the park. Asiatic Black Bear are still present and the tracks of perhaps two or three remaining Tigers are occasionally reported. Snakes are often seen, including Reticulate Python, Malayan Pit Viper, King Cobra and Malayan Krait.

At least 54 bird species have been reported in the park. Both the Great and Wreathed Hornbills are still present, along with Silver Pheasant, Thick-billed and Mountain Imperial Pigeons, Bay Owl, Long-tailed Broadbill, Blue Pitta, Asian Fairy-bluebird, Blue Whistling

Thrush and Sulphur-breasted Warbler. Wildlife is most likely to be seen in the less accessible valleys of the park, by trekking with a guide from the ranger station at Klong Pla Kang Waterfalls or along the trail to the summit of Khao Chamao, which branches off from the waterfall trail.

Caves

The main attraction of Khao Wong is its extensive collection of limestone caves, 12 kilometres (7½ miles) north of 'Km 286' on Highway 3. Of the 80 chambers present, 18 can be visited, although access can be dangerous in the rainy season, because the caves become flooded. A guide is therefore essential. The chambers are beautifully decorated with stalagmites, stalactites and sparkling crystals.

Nature Trails

Walkers can choose from among six short nature trails, starting from the park headquarters and leading to waterfalls, viewpoints and salt licks. A longer educational trail now links the park headquarters with the ranger station at Klong Pla Kang Waterfall, 4 kilometres (2½ miles) to the north. Access to the trail is allowed only with a guide from the park headquarters who provides commentary (in Thai) about medicinal and other useful plants along the way. A tough trek to the summit of Khao Chamao and from there to Khao Wong is also possible.

Far left: *The Malayan Krait can be found on the forest floor from the base to the summit of Khao Chamao. It goes hunting for other snakes at night.*

Left: *The Asian Fairy-bluebird is resident at higher elevations on Khao Chamao, preferring evergreen forest habitats. It sometimes forms flocks when feeding in fruiting trees.*

Left: *Banteng spend the day in deep forest but emerge into open areas at night to feed primarily on grasses and herbs. They usually live in herds of five to 25 individuals.*

KHAO LAEM NATIONAL PARK

A Remnant of the Western Forests

Preserving a remnant of the vast, dense forests that formerly blanketed the western province of Kanchanaburi, Khao Laem National Park forms part of the Western Forest Complex, a collection of national parks and wildlife sanctuaries that protect the largest area of continuous forest in Southeast Asia. Khao Laem offers visitors attractive guided forest walks and an opportunity to explore a vast reservoir and its many inlets and islands by boat. The park was declared in 1991 to conserve 1,497 square kilometres (578 square miles) of the catchment area of the reservoir.

A Forest Walk along a Cascade

Although most of the forest at Khao Laem is in the process of recovering from intensive logging of dipterocarp trees in the late 20th century, it still retains visible populations of

Opposite, above: *One of the many meandering inlets to the Khao Laem Reservoir.*

Opposite, below left: *A young naturalist floats a huge leaf of the tree* Macaranga gigantea *on a pool of water.*

Opposite, below right: *Ramiflory, the production of fruits on trunks or branches, is common amongst figs.*

Above, right: Tacca chantrieri, *appropriately named the Black Bat Flower by local people, is toxic, but is also a valued ingredient in traditional remedies for several illnesses.*

many wildlife species. One of the best areas to see birds and mammals is around the park headquarters. There, park rangers guide visitors around a three-hour circular nature trail. Initially, the trail gradually ascends through evergreen forest, following a 23-tier cascade known as Namtok Kratenjeng, which tumbles over limestone rocks. White, orange and iridescent blue-and-green butterflies cluster around the many rock pools along the stream, and multicoloured land crabs are common, their numerous burrows pockmarking the trail in several places.

At dawn, White-handed Gibbons loudly proclaim their territories around the trail, whilst overhead the whooshing sounds of Great Hornbills in flight add variety to the morning concert as they navigate between the fig trees that are one of their most important food sources in this valley. Two rare pheasant species, Siamese Fireback and Kalij Pheasant, as well as commoner birds, including Blue Magpie and woodpeckers such as Greater and Common Flamebacks, occur in this forest. A comprehensive bird survey has not yet been carried out, so the total number of bird species in the national park is unknown. At night, fireflies are particularly abundant, whilst civets and Black Giant Squirrels emerge to gorge themselves on the numerous wild bananas that grow along the stream.

Common Barking Deer and Common Wild Pig can sometimes be seen. Serow are still fairly common, but

Location: In Kanchanaburi Province, northwest from Bangkok, near the border with Myanmar.

Climate: Monsoonal; wet season May–October; cool, dry season November–January (minimum temperature down to 10°C/50°F); hot, dry season February–April (maximum temperature up to 38°C/100°F).

When to Go: Any time of the year.

Access: From the provincial capital of Kanchanaburi, follow Highway 323 northwest for 147 km (92 miles), making a sharp right turn just before Tong Pha Phum. The park headquarters is east of the road, accessible via a short dirt track. The public bus service between Kanchanaburi and Sangkla Buri can drop visitors near the headquarters.

Permits: None required.

Equipment: Precautions against malaria essential; tough shoes and light clothing for jungle walks; sunscreen and hat for boat trips.

Facilities: Apart from a campsite at the park headquarters, no accommodation or food is available within the national park. Guesthouses, boat trips on the reservoir and other modest tourist facilities are available at Sangkla Buri and there is a restaurant at Krung Kra Wia; guided nature trails from the park headquarters and the Bung Krung Ka Wia substation. No information is available in English.

Watching Wildlife: Gibbons, hornbills and Serow; a wide variety of forest and water birds.

Visitor Activities: Forest walks and birdwatching, boat trips on the reservoir, river rafting.

are mainly confined to inaccessible limestone crags. Sambar Deer and Asiatic Black Bear are more elusive, whilst other large mammals, such as Asian Elephant, Tiger, Leopard and Malayan Tapir occasionally migrate into the park from Thung Yai Wildlife Sanctuary, which adjoins the park to the northeast. The western half of Khao Laem National Park is now completely cut off from the eastern section by the reservoir, making it inaccessible to large mammals migrating from the core areas of the Western Forest Complex.

Waterfalls

Four natural attractions are clustered around Krung Kra Wia, on Highway 323 approximately 10 kilometres (6 miles) south of the park headquarters. The gentle Krung Kra Wia Waterfalls and its popular restaurants provide a beauty spot at which to enjoy a picnic, but the nearby Daichong Waterfalls are more spectacular, with water crashing over granite rocks that have miraculously become colonized by trees. A few kilometres to the south, Krung Kra Wia Cave is reached via an unmarked footpath leading east from the main road. A guide from the Krung Kra Wia substation is essential to visit this 400-metre (1,312-foot) long cave, which has a stream running through it and is festooned with stalagmites and stalactites.

Bung Krung Kra Wia is a small marshy lake with reed beds where waterbirds are easily observed. The lake and its wildlife-viewing platform are the main attraction on a self-guided, circular, interpretive trail, which starts and finishes at the Bung Krung Kra Wia substation, on the main road a few kilometres south of Krung Kra Wia Waterfalls. Common birds around the lake include Chinese Pond Heron, Red-wattled Lapwing, Indian Roller, White-throated Kingfisher and Common Kingfisher.

Khao Laem Reservoir

The reservoir began forming in the early 1980s, following completion of a dam across the Khwae Noi River, south of the park near Thong Pha Phum. As water levels rose, the reservoir submerged an entire village. During the dry season, when the water level is low, the spires of the village's temple are revealed above the surface of the reservoir which, along with the emergent skeletal remains of drowned trees, create a surrealistic atmosphere to boat trips on the reservoir. Popular destinations for boat trips include the Sunyataram Forest Monastery, a meditation centre, and a large refugee camp for Mon people fleeing oppression in Myanmar. Near the dam, several operators offer raft trips down the Khwae Noi River as far as Sai Yok National Park and all the way to Kanchanaburi City.

KHAO LAEM YA–MU KO SAMET MARINE NATIONAL PARK

Popular Islands and Beaches

Since the early 1980s, Khao Laem Ya–Mu Ko Samet Marine National Park in the Gulf of Thailand has provided a haven for Bangkok's stressed-out office workers and students seeking a peaceful retreat from the hustle and bustle of city life. Long sandy beaches, fringed by coconut palms, calm sea, perfect for swimming, and remnants of coral reefs and forests are the main attractions. In addition, the park has become a famous battleground between opposing views on whether or not national parks should be developed for tourism.

Declared in 1981, the park protects only 8 square kilometres (3 square miles) of land; part of the coast of Rayong, including the headland called Khao Laem Ya where the headquarters is situated, the main island, Samet, and several small islands. The rest of the park (123 square kilometres, 47 square miles) is open ocean. Ko Samet is 6 kilometres (4 miles) long by 3 kilometres (2 miles) wide and features secluded sandy coves along its eastern shore.

Above, right: Palm trees are typical features of beachside scenery in Thailand.

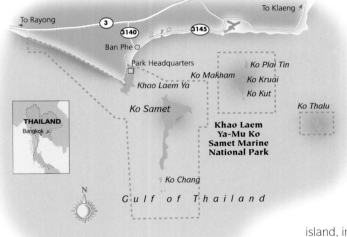

Beaches

It is the park's beaches, covered with some of the finest white sand in the country, that draw more than a quarter of a million visitors to Ko Samet each year. The sand is high in silica and, in the past, was dredged for glass production. Gently sloping into the Gulf of Thailand, and with a few colourful patches of coral still surviving, the beaches are perfect for swimming or simply relaxing beneath the coconut palms. The best beaches on Ko Samet are on the eastern side of the island, in tiny bays, each a few hundred metres long, separated by rocky headlands. On the mainland, there are also magnificent, but less famous, beaches. From the park headquarters at Khao Laem Ya, for example, a narrow sandy beach extends 12 kilometres (7 1/2 miles) to the west.

Marine Life

A lot of the coral close to the eastern shore of Ko Samet has been badly affected by untreated sewage flowing into the sea from the many bungalow resorts that are clustered along the eastern bays. Around the southern tip of the island, however, some good areas of coral remain. Better reefs and clear waters are to be found

Location: Rayong Province, 20 km (12 miles) east of the provincial capital.

Climate: Monsoonal, mean annual rainfall about 1,350 mm (53 in); mean annual temperature 30°C (86°F); monsoon May–October (11–17 rainy days per month) with strong winds and turbulent seas; cool season November–February (minimum temperature 9°C/48°F); hot, dry season March–May (maximum temperature 41°C/106°F).

When to Go: Any time, but avoid the monsoon season, weekends and public holidays.

Access: By road, follow Highway 3 east to Rayong. 20 km (12 miles) east of Rayong, turn south to Ban Phe. Buses from Bangkok's Eastern Bus Terminal run directly to the jetty at Ban Phe. The journey takes three or four hours. From Ban Phe, boats depart for Ko Samet between 8 a.m. and 5 p.m. at frequent intervals.

Permits: An entrance fee is charged.

Equipment: Protection against malaria; swimming gear; snorkel and mask.

Facilities: Ko Samet's beaches are lined with bungalows and restaurants; tour agencies operate boats to outlying islands.

Watching Wildlife: Coral reefs and fish; seabirds.

Visitor Activities: Relaxing on beaches; swimming and snorkelling; boat trips.

around the small limestone islands to the east: the Ko Kut and Ko Thalu island groups, accessible by boat from Ko Samet. Porite corals flourish, although branched corals are rare. Brilliant blue Yellow-tailed Damselfish, parrot fish and Horned Trunkfish are common. Dynamite fishing and boat anchors have, however, taken their toll and the reefs of Ko Samet cannot be compared with those of the Andaman Sea.

Terrestrial Wildlife

Although none of the original vegetation remains, the park still supports some wildlife in the secondary forest and scrubland which now cover the interior of the islands and the headlands. Lesser Mouse Deer and Long-tailed Macaque are still present, as well as a colony of flying foxes on Ko Thalu. The islands also provide nesting sites for seabirds, particularly terns (Black-naped, Great Crested, Bridled and Roseate) and the Pacific Reef-egret. Other birds include Asian Barred Owlet, Zebra Dove, Blue-winged Pitta and Coppersmith Barbet.

Conservation and Conflict

This tiny national park has become a hotbed of controversy, with legal battles between the Royal Forest Department (RFD) and the owners of bungalow resorts on the island. After the park was 'discovered' by backpackers in the early 1980s, tourism development mushroomed, leading to accumulation of garbage and discharge of untreated sewage into the sea, threatening the last remaining corals. Strictly speaking, operating privately owned resorts in a national park is illegal, and the Royal Forest Department has attempted to close down the tourist resorts several times. Resort owners claim that they started their businesses before the island became a national park, whereas the RFD claims that encroachment occurred mostly after the area was declared a national park and that private businesses should not make a profit from national resources. Court orders, demanding dismantlement of 43 resorts, have been ignored. The latest attempt to solve this problem involves granting existing resort owners contracts, allowing them to rent their land from the RFD for 10 to 20 years, after which the land will be returned to the national park. Unless further tourism development on the island can be halted, Ko Samet is destined to become just another seaside resort, and its ecological value will be destroyed forever.

Above: *A Mushroom Coral washed up on one of Ko Samet's beaches. Mushroom Corals can survive in relatively turbid waters by shedding deposited sediment.*

Top, right: *The Zebra (or Peaceful) Dove can still be found amongst what remains of Ko Samet's scrubby vegetation.*

Right: *Very little of the original beach vegetation remains on Ko Samet, but a few large Pandanus treelets survive. Their seeds can be dispersed by ocean currents.*

KHAO SAM ROI YOT MARINE NATIONAL PARK

Coastal Marshes and Limestone Pinnacles

A diversity of habitats, striking scenery and spectacular caves are the main attractions of Khao Sam Roi Yot, Thailand's first marine national park. Declared in 1966, the park consists of a long, narrow, isolated, jagged limestone mountain, rising from an alluvial plain to 605 metres (1,947 feet) above sea level, overlooking coastal marshes and beaches. The precipitous topography has protected both forests and remnant mammal populations. Although the park was enlarged in 1982 to include internationally important freshwater marshes, it is still relatively small at only 98 square kilometres (38 square miles). There are two interpretations of the park's name. One refers to an ancient shipwreck, during which 300 Chinese sailors miraculously survived. A more literal translation is 'Mountain with 300 Peaks'. Visitors can enjoy a wide range of activities in the national park, including spotting rare migrant birds, boating through mangrove forest, scrambling through awe-inspiring caves, or merely relaxing on a tropical sandy beach.

Opposite: The coastal wetlands of Khao Sam Roi Yot are of international importance for bird conservation, but the park is also one of the most endangered in Thailand.

Above, right: The Purple Heron prefers to frequent the more secluded parts of Khao Sam Roi Yot's coastal wetlands for stalking fish.

Marshlands of International Importance

Khao Sam Roi Yot is of particular interest to ornithologists. At least 316 bird species have been recorded in the park, of which 150 are migrants. Near the village of Rong Jai, on the inland side of the mountain, are the best lowland coastal marshes in Thailand, consisting of reed beds, and a network of small pools and canals, which offer both security and open water to visiting birds. The marshes provide an excellent opportunity to observe large water birds, songbirds and raptors. The area is one of only two sites in Thailand where the Purple Heron breeds. Common resident water birds include the Lesser Whistling-duck, Cotton Pygmy-goose, Yellow Bittern, Black Bittern, Pheasant-tailed Jacana, Little Grebe, Little Cormorant and the Purple Swamphen.

The marshes provide a crucial refuge for winter migrants, flying south from China and Siberia to escape the cold, including several species of duck (of which Garganey is the most common), Grey Heron, Eurasian Marsh and Pied Harriers, Greater Spotted and Imperial Eagles, and passerines.

The IUCN *Directory of Asian Wetlands* ranks the site as globally important. Despite international recognition of the park's conservation value, however, it is one of the most threatened conservation areas in Thailand. Sadly, drainage and pollution have severely reduced the quantity and quality of water in the marshlands. Poaching of water birds, burning of reed beds, uncontrolled cattle

Location: 63 km (39 miles) south of Hua Hin, in the province of Prachuab Khiri Khan.

Climate: One of the driest areas of Thailand. Mean annual rainfall is only about 1,000 mm (39 in). Most rain falls during the southwest monsoon, May–October, when high winds can occur. Dry season December–March. Mean annual temperature 27°C (81°F).

When to Go: December to March is best for winter bird migrants. The park becomes very crowded during public holidays.

Access: By car from Bangkok, follow Highway 4 to Pranburi. Turn left at Pranburi crossroads and follow the signs 25 km (40 miles) to the park entrance, then another 14 km (22½ miles) to the headquarters. Public buses from Bangkok to Pranburi, where motorcycle taxis or local buses can be hired.

Permits: An entrance fee is charged.

Equipment: Precautions against mosquitoes are essential; a torch for exploring caves; swimming gear for beaches.

Facilities: Bungalows and tents for rent at the park headquarters, Laem Sala Beach and Sam Phraya Beach; restaurants at headquarters and beaches; visitor centre and exhibition; boat trips; several nature trails. Private resorts offer accommodation near Bang Pu.

Watching Wildlife: Serow, Dusky Langur, a wide range of water birds, limestone flora and mangrove forests.

Visitor Activities: Birdwatching, swimming and relaxing on beaches, exploring caves, boat trips through mangrove forest.

Map labels: To Hua Hin; Phetkasem Road; THAILAND; Bangkok; Gulf of Thailand; Viewpoint; Rong Jai; Viewpoint; Sam Roi Yot; Bang Pu; Kaeo Cave; Laem Sala Beach; Phraya Nakon Cave; Sai Cave; Kluang Tanot; Khao Sam Roi Yot Marine National Park; Sam Phraya Beach; Visitor Centre; Khao Daeng Park Headquarters; To Phetkasem Road; N

grazing and the conversion of large areas into shrimp farms have severely damaged the area. It would be an international tragedy if this situation were allowed to continue.

A Diversity of Shorebirds

Shorebirds are an added attraction for birdwatchers at Khao Sam Roi Yot. No other comparable coastal site supports more species within such a small area. On mudflats, common waders include Common Redshank, Common Greenshank, Marsh Sandpiper and Broad-billed Sandpiper. Spoon-billed Sandpipers and Little Stints can sometimes be observed among flocks of Rufous-necked Stints. Along sandy beaches, Greater Sand Plovers, Bar-tailed Godwits, Sanderlings and Terek Sandpipers are commonly seen. Little Terns and Malaysian Plovers nest on beaches above the high-tide

mark, although disturbance by tourists, egg stealing and trampling by cattle undoubtedly destroy many nests.

Mammals on View

Tool-using monkeys provide an intriguing spectacle along the shoreline of Ko Khoram, one of several small islands within the national park. At low tide, Long-tailed Macaques scour the rocks for shellfish. The monkeys grasp small rocks, using them as hammers to crack open the shells and gain access to the nutritious meat inside. This unusual sight can be observed from boats hired from local fishermen. Visitors are not allowed to land on the island or to feed the monkeys, to avoid disturbing this unique behaviour.

Khao Sam Roi Yot is one of the best places to see another primate, the Dusky Langur. This delightful black-and-white monkey can easily be observed, moving

Above: *The Spot-billed Pelican is one of many endangered bird species that find refuge in the coastal marshes of Khao Sam Roi Yot.*

Far left: *A Long-tailed Macaque forages for crabs amongst the roots of mangrove trees. This monkey is also known as the Crab-eating Macaque.*

Left: *Scrubby vegetation clings miraculously to sheer cliffs.*

through the mangrove trees around the park headquarters in the late afternoon.

The largest mammal surviving in the park is the Serow. This black goat-like animal is superbly adapted to live in steep terrain. Serows can be seen in late evening or early morning by scanning the limestone crags with binoculars. For a closer view, follow the path from the park headquarters to the Khao Daeng viewpoint. The Serow population in the national park appears to be fairly stable at around 50 individuals.

More elusive among the parks 14 confirmed mammal species are Common Barking Deer, Common Wild Pig, Banded Linsang, Fish-eating Cat, Malayan Pangolin, Malayan Porcupine, Leopard Cat, Slow Loris and possibly Leopard. Small-clawed Otters can sometimes be seen chasing fish in marshlands and mangroves.

Magnificent Caves

Undoubtedly the most impressive geological features of the park are its caves the most famous of which is Phraya Nakon Cave. This cave consists of two vast caverns, open to the sky, with trees growing inside. Three of

Above: *The Common Flameback, a type of woodpecker, inhabits open woodlands. Look out for this species when boating through mangrove forest.*

Right: *The magnificent Phraya Nakon cavern is open to the sky, allowing trees to thrive inside. The royal pavilion was built for the visit of King Rama V in 1896.*

Thailand's kings have visited the cave and a royal pavilion, constructed for a visit by King Rama V in 1896, adds a majestic air to what is already an awesome natural feature. The pavilion is the symbol of Prachuab Khiri Khan. The cave is accessed from the small fishing village of Bang Pu. From there, a limestone promontory is traversed by a steep, but well-made, path leading down to Laem Sala Beach. Alternatively boats can be hired to ferry visitors around the promontory. From the beach, a further steep climb taking about half an hour leads to the cave's entrance.

Sai and Kaeo Caves are also worth a visit. Although smaller than Phraya Nakon, they are more highly decorated with stalactites, stalagmites and 'petrified waterfalls'. Guides with lanterns lead visitors to view glittering calcite crystals.

Left, above: *Egrets are common residents in the paddyfields and freshwater marshes around the park.*

Left, below: *Limestone cliffs are a dominate feature of the coastal marshes.*

Below: *The Dusky Langur is common in the mangrove forests around the park headquarters. This monkey is also called the Spectacled Langur due to the prominent white rings around its eyes.*

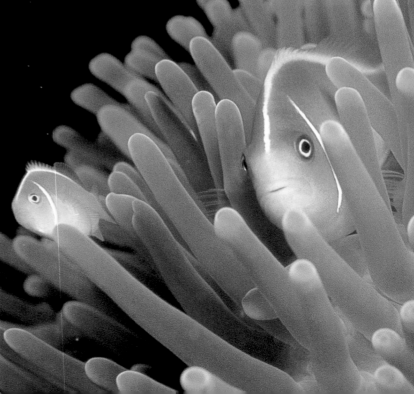

Mu Ko Chang Marine National Park

Forests, Coral Reefs and Shipwrecks

Despite being declared a National Marine Park in 1982, Ko Chang has become one of the fastest-developing beach resort islands in the Gulf of Thailand. Situated in Thailand's easternmost province of Trat, close to the Cambodian border, the park includes 85 per cent of the main island, Ko Chang, and 46 smaller islands, totalling 192 square kilometres (76 square miles) of land and 458 square kilometres (177 square miles) of sea. At more than 30 kilometres (19 miles) long and 14 kilometres (9 miles) wide and rising to a maximum elevation of 743 metres (2,438 feet), Ko Chang is Thailand's second largest island (after Phuket).

Opposite, above: Tourism development along the west coast of Ko Chang has already laid claim to most of the beaches, which have been excluded from the national park.

Opposite, below left: From tranquil sandy beaches to mountains cloaked in forest, Ko Chang supports a range of attractions for nature tourists.

Opposite, below right: These Pink Skunk Anemonefish find a refuge from predators amongst the stinging tentacles of a sea anemone. Somehow, they are immune to its stings.

Above, right: The Green Imperial Pigeon has been considerably reduced in numbers all over Thailand due to hunting, but on Ko Chang the species finds a refuge.

Unfortunately, the beaches along the western coast of Ko Chang and several other islands have been excluded from the park and are undergoing a tourism development boom, similar to that which transformed Phuket and Samui in the 1980s. More than 70 per cent of Ko Chang's hilly interior is, however, still covered in dense primary ever-green forest, of a particular type that is restricted to southeast Thailand and Cambodia. High annual rainfall feeds several beautiful waterfalls. Offshore, coral reefs are accessible by snorkellers, whilst sunken World War II battleships provide an additional attraction for scuba divers.

Naval History

Ko Chang is famous for being the location of the only naval battle in Thai military history. In Salak Phet Bay, at the southern end of Ko Chang, on 17 January 1941, three Thai warships, the *Songkhla*, the *Chonburi* and the *Thonburi*, confronted seven French cruisers during a dispute as to whether the islands belonged to Thailand or French-colonized Cambodia. Although the French ships were repulsed, both the *Songkhla* and the *Chonburi* were sunk, and many sailors drowned. The Royal Thai Navy commemorates the event every year on the anniversary of the battle. The *Thonburi*, now lying 200 metres out

Location: In the Gulf of Thailand, 8 km (5 miles) south-west from Trat Province coast.

Climate: Dry season November–May; rainy season June–October; average annual rainfall 3,200 mm (126 in), wettest August (690 mm/27 in), driest December (no rainfall); hottest April (mean maximum 34°C/93°F); coldest January and February (mean minimum 22°C/72°F).

When to Go: December to March. Open all year around, but access difficult during rainy season. Accommodation fully booked during public holidays.

Access: By boat from three mainland piers: Tha Ferry Ko Chang (at Aow Thammachat car ferry), Tha Ko Chang Centre Point and Tha Laem Ngop. A road provides motor-vehicle access to most of the beach areas. Shared taxis run sporadically.

Permits: Entrance fees are charged at waterfalls. Contact the park headquarters opposite the police station near Laem Ngop Pier to arrange your visit.

Equipment: For forest walks, light clothes and strong boots; for beaches, sunblock, scuba or snorkelling equipment; protection against endemic strains of malaria.

Facilities: Resorts along all beaches; camping at Khlong Plu and Than Mayom waterfalls; many restaurants; local long-tailed boats or speedboats for hire; diving centres at Haad Sai and Kai Bai Beaches.

Watching Wildlife: Common corals and marine fish, sea turtles, hornbills and monkeys.

Visitor Activities: Usual beach activities, diving and snorkelling, visiting waterfalls and forest walks.

Below: *A diver floats above a bed of staghorn corals. The waters around Ko Chang are some of the clearest in the Gulf of Thailand.*

from a river mouth, at a depth of 15 metres (50 feet), encrusted with sponges and corals and home to a great variety of fish species, is a popular site with scuba divers.

Coral Reefs

Although no match for the clarity of the Andaman Sea, the waters around Ko Chang are among the clearest in the Gulf, with visibility as high as 10 metres (33 feet). Coral reefs in sheltered areas, mainly around the smaller islands and along the eastern shore of Ko Chang, attract snorkellers and scuba divers. Reefs of massive staghorn, laminar and columna coral provide habitat for Giant Clams, sea anemones, sea fans, sea stars and many fish species. White-tip and Reef Sharks are also fairly common. Divers occasionally encounter Hawksbill Turtles, which lay their eggs around Ko Rang. Local boats can be hired from most of the Ko Chang beaches to visit the best reefs around Ko Rang, Ko Lao Klang, Ko Lao Ya and Ko Wai. Regular ferries from Laem Ngop serve some of the smaller islands, where resort accommodation is sometimes available.

Dense Forest

One of the charms of this park is the close proximity between a rich and varied marine environment and relatively undisturbed evergreen forest – perhaps the most extensive and best-preserved forest on any of the Gulf islands. On Ko Chang, several massive *Dipterocarpus* species, *Anisoptera costata* and *Hopea odorata* trees tower above the main forest canopy. With more than 3,000 mm (118 inches) of rainfall each year, the structure and lushness of the forest approaches that of equatorial rainforest. Although the fauna of the forest is not especially diverse, it is home to at least one endemic species, the Ko Chang Frog. Among a total of 41 other reptile or amphibian species are Soft-shelled Turtle, Water Monitor, Reticulated Python and King Cobra. At least 74 bird species have been observed, including Shikra, Red-headed Trogon, Green Imperial Pigeon, three hornbill species (Wreathed, Oriental Pied and Great), Tickell's Blue Flycatcher and Heart-spotted Woodpecker. Two species of pitta (Blue-winged and Hooded) advertise their presence in the forest by distinctive whistling calls at dawn and dusk.

Apart from thriving troops of Stump-tailed Macaques, mammals in the park are rarely seen. Fortunate visitors might, however, encounter Common Wild Pig, Common Barking Deer, Small Indian Civet and Variable Squirrel. The best points from which to start exploring the forest are Than Mayom Waterfall near the main ranger station on the eastern side of Ko Chang, and Khlong Phlu waterfall on the western side. A very steep footpath connects the two waterfalls, traversing the granite hills that run the length of the island. The walk takes a full day and should be attempted only with a guide.

Right: *Hawksbill Turtles are endangered due to collection of their eggs and marine pollution, but a few still nest on the more remote islands of Mu Ko Chang National Park.*

SAI YOK NATIONAL PARK

Home of the World's Smallest Bat

Travelling west from the city of Kanchanaburi the scenery becomes dominated by limestone karst. Soaring pinnacles and craggy cliffs touch the clouds, providing spectacular views. One of the largest areas of karst, to the west of Highway 323, is Sai Yok National Park, rising to a maximum elevation of 1,327 metres (4,353 feet). The park features some of the most popular waterfalls in the country, and several spectacular caves, reached by boat or forest trails. It is home to the world's smallest bat and retains historical relics from World War II. The park was declared in 1980 and covers an area or 500 square kilometres (193 square miles).

Kitti's Hog-nosed Bat

In October 1973, Mr Kitti Thonglongya was collecting bats in a cave at Sai Yok when he discovered a bat with no tail, unlike anything he had seen before. Weighing barely two grams, it was about the size of a large bumble bee. Not only had he discovered the world's smallest bat (possibly the world's smallest mammal), but the single representative of a family of bats new to science. Unfortunately, Mr Kitti Thonglongya died the following year, but Mr John Edwards Hill at the British Museum

Above, right: Discovered at Sai Yok, the Kitti's Hog-nosed Bat is probably the smallest mammal in the world.

(Natural History) published a description of the new species and family in 1974, from Mr Kitti's specimens. He named the species *Craseonycteris thonglongyai* (Family Craseonycteridae). These bats live in small colonies, deep inside the limestone caves that riddle Sai Yok National Park. They emerge from the caves at dusk to catch insects around the tops of trees and clumps of bamboo. At least 12 other bat species have been recorded in the park, including the Common Flying Fox, the largest in the world.

Mammals are rather difficult to see at Sai Yok, requiring challenging treks over precipitous topography. Some of the commoner of the 50 or so mammal species recorded in the national park include White-handed Gibbon, Stump-tailed and Long-tailed Macaques, Sambar Deer, Common Barking Deer, Malayan Porcupine, Serow, Slow Loris and Common Wild Pig. Asian Elephants migrate seasonally into the park and can sometimes be seen near Ranger Station 4. Tiger, Leopard and most of the smaller cats are all still relatively common in the park.

Another wildlife feature of Sai Yok National Park is the endemic Regal Crab (*Thaipusa sirikit,* named after Thailand's current Queen). These brilliant purple-white-and-red crustaceans live near streams all year round.

At least 141 bird species occur in the national park, including three hornbill species and rarities such as the White-rumped Falcon and the Spotted Wood-owl.

Location: In Kanchanaburi Province, about 100 km (6½ miles) west of the provincial capital.

Climate: Monsoonal; mean annual rainfall approximately 1,150 mm (45 in); rainy season May–October; cool, dry season November–February (monthly rainfall less than 20 mm/ 1 inch); hot, dry season March–May (mean monthly temperatures approximately 30°C/86°F).

When to Go: Cool season for forest treks; rainy season for rafting. Extremely crowded at weekends and public holidays.

Access: Follow Highway 323, west from Kanchanaburi, for about 100 km (62 miles). The park headquarters is reached via a dirt track running west a few km from the main road. Public bus services from Kanchanaburi to Sangkhla Buri pass by the entrance to the headquarters.

Permits: An entrance fee is charged.

Equipment: Protection against malaria advisable; light clothing and boots for jungle treks; a torch for caves; swimming gear.

Facilities: Park bungalows and privately owned floating accommodation for rent; camping, restaurants, exhibition and nature trails at the park headquarters.

Watching Wildlife: Birds, bats and other small mammals.

Visitor Activities: Forest walks; river rafting; exploring caves.

Above: *Giant* Alocasia macrorhizos *leaves struggle to absorb light in the dim understorey of dense forest near a limestone stream.*

Relics of World War II

During World War II the Japanese occupied the area. In 1942, to secure Burma, they began constructing the 415-kilometre (259-mile) 'death railway'. More than 250,000 Asian labourers and 60,000 prisoners of war were forced to construct the railway, using hand tools. Approximately 90,000 people died during this endeavour. A short section of the railway, passing through the park, has been restored and now forms part of a nature trail. Cooking stoves, used to prepare meals for Japanese soldiers, have also been preserved.

Waterfalls

Right: *A Buddhist shrine inside Rawa cave. Accessible by road or river boat, this 530-m long cave has several chambers up to 25 m high and is a favoured roosting site of the Great Roundleaf Bat.*

Although small, the waterfalls are the most popular tourist attraction of the park. Small tributaries of the Khwae Noi tumble over a limestone shelf, which forms the eastern bank of the river. Short boat rides on the main river provide the best views of the falls. During the rainy season, when the river level rises, the falls are almost submerged. The area around the falls is highly developed with concrete paths and food concessions. Paddling in the waterfalls is allowed, but swimming in the main river is forbidden because of the powerful current.

River Rafting

Sai Yok is a starting point for river-rafting trips, which can take visitors downstream as far as Kanchanaburi. Unfortunately, the rafting industry has grown out of control. At weekends and holidays the river becomes choked with rafts, which block views of the waterfalls and destroy the tranquillity that was once the park's main attraction.

Left: *Immortalized in a famous folk song and visited by King Rama V, the waterfalls of Sai Yok attract hundreds of thousands of visitors annually.*

Below, left: *The White-crested Laughingthrush is a common resident throughout western and northern Thailand. It is an exceptional songster, and for this reason is often captured for the pet industry.*

Below: *The brilliantly coloured Regal Crab, a recently discovered new species. It is a speciality of Sai Yok, being restricted in its distribution to a single river within the national park.*

NORTHERN THAILAND

With mountain ranges, misty valleys, the country's tallest waterfalls and the highest regional forest cover (43.5 per cent), northern Thailand is a rewarding destination for naturalists. The northern mountains support at least 150 mammal species and 383 birds. Chiang Mai University's Herbarium holds records for 3,450 vascular plants from the north.

Most of the northern parks are centred on individual mountains (*doi*) such as Doi Khuntan and Doi Suthep-Pui, featuring hill walks and birdwatching. Doi Inthanon National Park includes Thailand's highest mountain and unique high altitude forest types.

The northern forests protect watersheds that feed the Chao Phraya River and supply water to the nation's capital. At Khlong Lan, waterfalls attract thousands of tourists annually. A man-made reservoir provides the central focus at Sri Lanna, whilst the Ping River, gliding between towering limestone cliffs, is the principle attraction at Mae Ping National Park.

Man has influenced northern Thailand's forests for millennia. At Ob Luang ancient graves and rock paintings date back thousands of years. More recently, the forests were logged for teak, and an area recovering from such devastation can be seen at Mae Wong.

At least 10 ethnic minorities, known as 'hill tribes', have settled in Thailand's northern highlands. Each tribe has distinctive traditions, costumes and agricultural practices. Hill-tribe villages in many of the northern parks often welcome tourists (e.g. Nam Tok Mae Surin, Doi Suthep-Pui, Doi Inthanon).

Over most of northern Thailand, large mammals have long been hunted out, but in the lower northern region, at Nam Nao and Thung Salaeng Luang, Asian Elephants, deer and wild cattle can still be seen.

DOI INTHANON NATIONAL PARK

Thailand's Highest Mountain

Situated in the province of Chiang Mai, Doi Inthanon National Park protects Thailand's highest mountain, along with the greatest diversity of forest types and bird species found in any single park in the country. Rising to a maximum elevation of 2,776 metres (9,108 feet) above sea level and covering an area of 482 square kilometres (186 square miles), the park is one of the most famous birdwatching sites in Thailand, especially during the cool season, when rare winter migrants are a speciality.

Formerly known as Doi Angka, the name of the mountain was changed in 1889 to a shortened version of the name of Chiang Mai's last monarch, King Inthawichayanon, whose ashes are interred in a small stupa near the summit. Doi Inthanon was declared a national park in 1972.

Opposite: Wachiratan is just one of many spectacular waterfalls that thunder down Thailand's highest mountain.

Above, right: Doi Inthanon is famous for its rhododendrons, both red and white. Rhododendron vietchianum *flowers mainly in January.*

Previous pages:
Page 60: The North is Thailand's most heavily forested region. Page 61: Intriguing customs and colourful costumes of hill-tribe people add cultural diversity to Thailand's Northern Region.

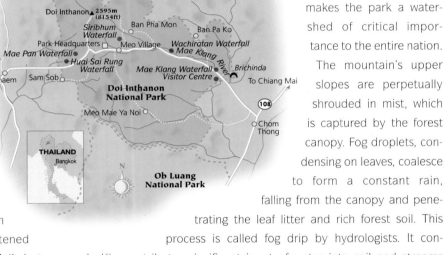

The Gift of Water

Doi Inthanon forms the watershed between the Ping River to the east and the Chaem River to the west, both of which eventually feed the Chao Phraya River, which supplies water to rice farms of the central plains and to Bangkok. This makes the park a watershed of critical importance to the entire nation.

The mountain's upper slopes are perpetually shrouded in mist, which is captured by the forest canopy. Fog droplets, condensing on leaves, coalesce to form a constant rain, falling from the canopy and penetrating the leaf litter and rich forest soil. This process is called fog drip by hydrologists. It contributes significant input of water into soil and streams that would not occur without the forest. Thai folklore, on the other hand, provides a simpler explanation: the mountain is said to be the home of 'the spirit who shares water'.

Thundering Waterfalls

Doi Inthanon's high rainfall provides a plentiful year-round supply of water for some spectacular waterfalls. Mae Klang Waterfall, near the park entrance, attracts huge numbers of visitors, who come to swim, picnic and relax by the thunderous falls. Wachiratan Waterfall plummets 50 metres (164 feet) in a single leap over a sheer granite cliff, with a roar that local people compare with a stampede of elephants. The most spectacular waterfall in the park is Mae Ya, arguably the tallest in Thailand. Water tumbles over hundreds of small steps, a total of 250 metres (820 feet).

Location: Chiang Mai Province, about 100 km (62 miles) southwest of the provincial capital.

Climate: Monsoonal; above 1,000 m (3,281 ft), annual rainfall exceeds 2,500 mm (98 in); rainy season May–October; cool season November–February, with frosts (minimum temperature 8°C/18°F); hot, dry season February–April.

When to Go: December to March are the best months for birds; very crowded during holidays and weekends.

Access: By car from Chiang Mai City, follow Highway 108 southwest. At Km 58, just before Chom Thong, turn west on Highway 1009, 8 km (3 miles) to the park entrance. Public buses run from Chiang Mai to Chom Tong and local shared pickup-truck taxis from Chom Thong into the park.

Permits: An entrance fee is charged.

Equipment: Warm clothing and waterproof gear is essential when visiting the summit; protection against malaria; hiking boots; binoculars.

Facilities: A metalled road runs to the summit; bungalows for rent and camping facilities; three visitor information centres; small restaurants; nature trails and guided walks.

Watching Wildlife: Birds and plants are the main attractions; orchids, rhododendrons, parasitic plants; Green-tailed Sunbird, Ashy-throated Warbler.

Visitor Activities: Birdwatching and photography; mountain and forest walks; visiting waterfalls and hill-tribe villages.

A Diversity of Forests

Below 1,000 metres (3,281 feet) elevation, Doi Inthanon supports deciduous dipterocarp forest, bamboo deciduous forest and mixed deciduous forest that are all fairly typical of the lowlands of northern Thailand. Near the summit, however, the evergreen forest, with its abundance of woody lianas and epiphytes, constantly shrouded in mist, has a unique and enchanting atmosphere. Such epiphytes include brilliant green ferns and mosses, dangling lichens, and a profusion of orchids and other flowering plants. The tree flora is characterized by families more usually associated with temperate climes (e.g. Fagaceae, Magnoliaceae, Theaceae, Ericaceae and Lauraceae).

Amongst the leaf litter, several curious parasitic plants grow. Looking more like the fruiting body of a fungus than a flowering plant, *Balanophora fungosa* forms tubers on the roots of oaks and other tree species. The fabulous *Sapria himalayana* is a member of the family Rafflesiaceae, famous for the largest flowers in the world. Although no match for such giants, the flowers of *S. himalayana* can reach 18 centimetres (7 inches) in diameter; 10-pointed red stars with yellow spots, feeding on the roots of lianas. A rhododendron, *Rhododendron arborea var. delavyi*, producing red blooms during December to February, is a speciality, and two white-flowering rhododendron species also occur.

Above: Sapria himalayana *is a parasitic plant which grows on the roots of lianas of the grape family (Vitaceae). Only its flowers are visible above the leaf litter during the cool season.*

Right: *Doi Inthanon is very much a cultural landscape. Both Hmong and Karen hill tribes have settlements and agricultural land within the park.*

A Sphagnum Bog

Near the summit, a nature trail winds around another unique habitat: a tiny patch of bog composed of sphagnum moss. This area might once have been the small pond that gave the mountain its original name. One possible translation of *Angka* is 'Pool of Crows'. Natural succession has long since turned the pool into Thailand's only sphagnum bog. Cool temperatures and soils saturated with acidic water are the conditions necessary for development of the bog. Recently, however, it seems to be drying out, allowing invasion by shrubs and trees. If this continues, Thailand will lose its only remaining patch of this habitat.

Unique Fauna

The evergreen forest that grows on the summit of Doi Inthanon has been isolated from other areas of similar habitat by vast lowlands for millions of years. Such isolation allows evolution of new subspecies, and eventually species. Doi Inthanon is home to an endemic subspecies of the Common European White-toothed

Far left: Arisaema erubescens *is common around the bog near the summit of Doi Inthanon.*

Left: *Fungi are an important component of northern forest ecosystems. They help to break down dead plant matter and recycle nutrients.*

Below: *Wild Piglets, one of the larger of the 66 mammal species recorded for Doi Inthanon. Hunting and forest destruction have all but wiped out most other large mammals.*

Right: *Trees encrusted with epiphytes of every description, including ferns, mosses, liverworts and especially orchids, lend a unique character to the upper forests of Doi Inthanon.*

Below: *The Golden Orbweave Spider spins incredibly strong, sticky, yellow, webs between trees in deciduous forest at lower elevations. Such webs can entrap very large insects, and sometimes even small birds and bats.*

Shrew, distinguished from other subspecies by its unique teeth. Like other shrews, they eat mainly insects, but the subspecies on Doi Inthanon also feeds on small mice and fledglings of ground-nesting birds. The subspecies of the Green-tailed Sunbird on Doi Inthanon is also endemic. Metallic green with a yellow-and-red breast, this very attractive little bird is often so tame that it almost appears to pose for photographs near the summit. Another species restricted in Thailand to Doi Inthanon is the Ashy-throated Warbler, which is common in evergreen forest above 2,000 metres (6,562 feet).

Thailand's Premier Birdwatching Site

With a bird list of 386 confirmed species, greater than any other conservation area in Thailand, Doi Inthanon is undoubtedly Thailand's foremost attraction for bird-watchers. Such diversity is due to the park's wide range of elevations, its variety of habitats and strategic position on migration routes.

The mountain is important not only for its diversity of birds, but also for rarities and first records, such as the Scaly-sided Merganser, one of the rarest and least-studied ducks in the world, and the Japanese Thrush. In the cool season, ornithologists flock to Doi Inthanon to record rare winter visitors, such as Speckled Wood-pigeon, Blue-fronted Redstart, Golden Bush-robin, Rosy Pipit, Collared Grosbeak and Tristram's Bunting, as well as various thrushes (Eye-browed, Grey-sided and Dusky). Notable resident birds include Rufous-throated Partridge, Ashy Wood-pigeon, Green and Purple Cochoas, Rufous-winged Buzzard, White-rumped Falcon, White-tailed Robin, Plumbeous Redstart, Dark-sided Thrush and Yellow-bellied Fantail.

Recently villagers, collaborating with park officers, have begun an eco-tourism service, with overnight stays in the traditional Karen village of Ban Mae Klang Luang (Km 26) and guided treks to see the birds. This enterprise has encouraged the villagers to stop hunting and adopt more sustainable agricultural practices to preserve the birds' habitats.

Left: *The Crocodile Salamander is known from only four locations in Thailand, but is still fairly common on Doi Inthanon.*

Below, Left: *With its trees festooned with dangling lichens and mosses, the forest on Doi Inthanon has its own unique atmosphere.*

Below, right: *The Green-tailed Sunbird is a speciality of Doi Inthanon, and is easily seen near the summit. The subspecies which lives there is endemic to the mountain.*

DOI KHUNTAN NATIONAL PARK

Railway Tunnel and Mountain Hike

Mountain hikes, ascending through different forest types, and railway history are the main attractions of Doi Khuntan National Park. Established in March 1975, this park protects 255 square kilometres (98 square miles) of forested hills, reaching a maximum elevation of 1,363 metres (4,472 feet) in the northern provinces of Lampoon and Lampang.

The Railway Tunnel

Doi Khuntan is the only national park in Thailand that has its own railway station. Coming from Bangkok, train

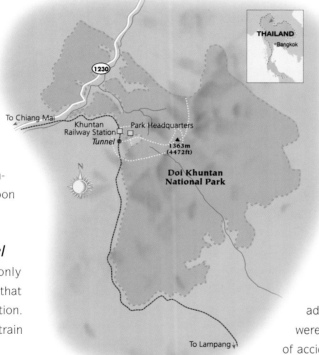

passengers travel through a 1.3-kilometre (almost 1 mile) tunnel, Thailand's longest, before emerging at Khuntan railway station, from where tracks and hiking trails lead to the park headquarters and the mountain summit.

The granite rocks of Doi Khuntan presented a formidable barrier to railway engineers attempting to link Bangkok with Chiang Mai. Construction of the tunnel began in 1907 and was completed in 1918, but at a terrible cost. More than a 1,000 labourers, mostly opium addicts from northeast Thailand, were stricken with malaria or died of accidents or suffocation in the terrible working conditions; a few were carried away by Tigers. A monument in front of the tunnel is dedicated to all those who died during its construction. The monument contains the ashes of Emil Eisenhofer, a German railway engineer instrumental in the tunnel's construction. The State Railways of Thailand still maintain a bungalow (known as Yaw 1) 900 metres (2,950 feet) above the station, originally used to house officers when the tunnel was being built, but now used to accommodate visitors to the national park.

Deciduous Forest

From the station, the trek to the summit is 8.3 kilometres (5 miles) and takes a full day. Hikers first pass

Opposite, top left: Once common throughout Thailand, the Three-striped Palm Civet is now scarce.

Opposite, centre left: The Tailed Green Jay is a common butterfly on the wing throughout the year.

Opposite, below left: This is Gomphostemma strobilinum, a stemless perennial herb. Variegated leaves are a feature amongst plants growing on the forest floor.

Opposite, right: Bamboo deciduous forest and folded mountains, a typical view from Doi Khuntan.

Above, right: The violet flowers of Impatiens violiflorae provide colour amongst the leaf litter of the evergreen forest.

Location: In the provinces of Lampang and Lampoon, midway between the two provincial capitals.

Climate: Monsoonal; mean annual rainfall 1,034 mm (41 in); mean annual temperature 26°C (79°F); rainy season July–October; cool dry season November–February (minimum temperature 5°C/41°F); hot, dry season March–June (maximum temperatures 38°C/100°F).

When to Go: The cool season provides comfortable temperatures for trekking.

Access: By train from Bangkok or Chiang Mai, on the northern railway line. By car, from Chiang Mai, follow the superhighway south to Lampoon. From there, follow Highway 11, 19 km (12 miles) to Mae Tha, then turn north on a minor road and follow the signs to the park headquarters. The road deteriorates into a dirt track requiring a four-wheel-drive vehicle in the rainy season. The summit is accessible only on foot.

Permits: None required.

Equipment: Insect repellent; light clothes and stout boots for walking; warm clothes during the cool season, especially near the summit; waterproof gear for the rainy season.

Facilities: Bungalows for rent and campsites; a small exhibition and store at the park headquarters. Campers should bring their own food.

Watching Wildlife: Birds and plants are the main attractions; some small mammals, squirrels, civets, barking deer, and so on.

Visitor Activities: Hill walking; birdwatching, botanising and so on.

Right: *Several bungalows, both large and small, provide accommodation for visitors near the park headquarters.*

through deciduous dipterocarp forest, which covers about half the park, before ascending through pine forests and degraded evergreen forest near the summit. The trees of deciduous dipterocarp forest support many epiphytes, including orchids of the genera *Bulbophyllum*, *Cymbidium* and *Eria*, which tend to flower at the same time as most of the trees, towards the end of the hot dry season. The attractiveness of orchid blooms, however, makes them vulnerable to plant collectors, who sell them at the railway station and in local markets. Today, therefore, orchids are rather scarce in the lowland forests of the park.

Owing to its lack of attractive flowers, however, one epiphyte has managed to avoid the depredations of the plant collectors. *Dischidia major* produces swollen, hollow leaves, looking like green bananas clustered around tree branches. These modified leaves provide the perfect environment for ants to nest in. After a while, debris, dragged by the ants into the leaf cavities breaks down to form a crumbly soil. The plant then grows roots inside its own leaves to extract moisture and mineral nutrients from the remains of the ants' nests, thus overcoming the shortage of water, soil and nutrients that is faced by all epiphytic plants.

The deciduous forest of lower elevations today looks very different from the original vegetation. Much of the lowlands were originally covered by teak, which was logged out in the early part of the 20th century. Enormous numbers of *Shorea* trees were felled for the railway to make sleepers and bridges and to provide fuel. In addition, large areas were buried beneath the spoil dumped after tunnel construction. Frequent fires have subsequently prevented recovery of this forest.

Pines and Evergreen Forest

Higher up the mountain, the summit trail passes through some magnificent groves of swaying bamboos before climbing into evergreen forest. The latter is by far the most diverse habitat on the mountain, accounting for 46 per cent of the park's vascular flora (at least 591 species). The rainy season is the best time to see flowers amongst the ground flora. In addition to many species of ginger, lily and ground orchid, the ground flora includes medicinal plants, such as *Orthosiphon spiralis*, traditionally used as a diuretic to clear kidney stones. An abundance of fungi attract mushroom collectors throughout the rainy season. Amongst the trees, Scarlet Minivets, Blue-winged Leafbirds, Blue-throated Barbets, Black-crested Bulbuls and Black-throated Sunbirds add colour to the forest canopy, whilst amongst the undergrowth a Blue Pitta may occasionally be seen.

One tree species in evergreen forest deserves special mention. During a floral survey of the mountain in 1994, J. F. Maxwell discovered the deciduous tree *Hovenia*

Left: *The epiphytic herb,* Aeschynanthus hosseusii *produces brilliant scarlet flowers from July to October, which are pollinated by sunbirds. The tiny seeds are as fine as dust and drift on the slightest breeze to find a suitable germination site on another tree.*

dulcis a new record for Thailand, at the southern limit of its distribution. Subsequently, research at Chiang Mai University's Forest Restoration Research Unit found that this species was ideal for planting in degraded areas to encourage recovery of natural forest ecosystems. It grows quickly, shades out weeds and attracts seed-dispersing birds, such as Wedge-tailed Pigeons, which feed in large numbers on its fleshy fruit stalks.

Pines are abundant in some areas. Both of Thailand's native pine species grow in the park (the two-needled pine, *Pinus merkusii,* and the three-needled pine, *P. kesiya*). *P. merkusii* is more common at mid elevations, with *P. kesiya* predominating around the summit area. Set amongst planted pines near the summit are bungalows built in the 1920s by missionaries, who retreated from the heat of the dry season to this cool, shady hill station. The accounts of the missionaries at that time speak of gibbons, hornbills, bears and monkeys in abundance, all sadly long gone. The missionary station, though, has survived.

Wildlife

Despite the damage caused by loggers and fires, the park still supports a remarkably high botanical diversity. Chiang Mai University Herbarium has specimens of nearly 1,300 species of vascular plant from Doi Khuntan, including 68 orchids, 35 gingers and 21 figs.

Large mammals have long been extirpated from the park, but smaller species still survive, including Siamese Hare, Slow Loris, Crestless Himalayan Porcupine, Common Tree-shrew and various species of squirrel, civet and marten. At least 183 bird species have been recorded within the park. Rare residents include Rufous-bellied Eagle, Giant Nuthatch and Green Cochoa, whilst the Grey-cheeked Warbler is a very rare winter visitor.

Below: *Looking more like a snake,* Ichthyophis kohtaoensis *is a Caecilian, a legless amphibian found in wet areas in lowland areas.*

DOI SUTHEP-PUI NATIONAL PARK

Temples and Waterfalls

It is said that tourists cannot claim to have really visited Chiang Mai, Thailand's northern capital, unless they make the pilgrimage to the famous temple, Wat Pratat, at the heart of Doi Suthep-Pui National Park. Constructed in 1372 or 1373 AD, the temple's golden chedi, which houses a relic of the Lord Buddha, dominates the city, glinting in the sunlight on a sub-peak of the mountain, surrounded by forest. The mountain is named after the 7th-century sage Vasudeva (also called Rishi Warsuthep), a central figure in local mythology, who lived in a cave on the mountain.

Doi Suthep-Pui National Park was created in 1981 to protect not only the surroundings of the temple, but also the diverse forest ecosystems of the mountain,

which provide a magnificent green backdrop to Chiang Mai city. The park consists of an isolated granite massif, with two main peaks. Doi Pui is the highest (1,685 metres, 5,528 feet), but the whole mountain is usually referred to as 'Doi Suthep', the secondary peak. Besides Wat Pratat, other cultural points of interest include the Hmong hill-tribe villages and Phuphing Palace, a favourite cool-season retreat for the royal family. The park is an important water catchment area, feeding streams that tumble over waterfalls, where they provide attractive picnic and campsites. A comprehensive survey of the park's flora, carried out by J. F. Maxwell at Chiang Mai University, has recorded at least 2,241 species of vascular plants. The park's diverse fauna includes at least 326 bird species, 500 butterflies, 300 moths, 61 mammals, 28 amphibians and 50 reptiles, all in a national park that covers just 261 square kilometres (101 square miles).

Deciduous Forests

For naturalists, the main interest of Doi Suthep is its diversity of forest types and birds. A walk on the mountain provides visitors with the most accessible introduction to the forest types of northern Thailand. The lower slopes

Opposite, left above: *Monthatharn Waterfall provides pleasant picnic sites and the opportunity for a cooling dip.*

Opposite, left centre: *At the end of the rainy season many ginger species produce brightly coloured infructescences.*

Opposite, left below: *The Little Pied Flycatcher is a very common resident in Doi Suthep's evergreen forest.*

Opposite, right: *A monk plants a tree to restore forest to a degraded area.*

Above, right: *The Golden-fronted Leafbird is one of three leafbird species that live on Doi Suthep.*

Location: Chiang Mai Province, bordering the western city limits of the provincial capital.

Climate: Monsoonal, mean annual rainfall approximately 1,000 mm (39 in) at the base of the mountain rising to nearly 2,000 mm (78 in) near the summit; rainy season May–October; cool, dry season November–January; hot dry season February–April (maximum temperature 40°C/104°F).

When to Go: Best during the cool season.

Access: The park starts at the end of Huaykaew Road in Chiang Mai City. Local pickup-truck taxis run from the city to Wat Pratat and beyond. A metalled road now runs all the way to the summit of Doi Pui.

Permits: None required. Entrance fees at waterfalls.

Equipment: Light clothes and boots for forest walks.

Facilities: Bungalows for rent at the park headquarters; small exhibition at Mae Sa Waterfalls.

Watching Wildlife: Birds and plants are the main attractions.

Visitor Activities: Forest walks; visiting waterfalls, hill-tribe villages and the mountain's famous temple Wat Pratat.

Right: *Common Barking Deer are the largest mammals remaining in the national park. Illegal hunters continue to shoot these beautiful animals, especially during the cool season.*

Below: *Doi Suthep is the home of many ancient spirits, some of which are thought to protect Chiang Mai from harm. Offerings to the spirits take many forms.*

are covered in deciduous dipterocarp-oak forest, composed of widely spaced trees: an abundance of *Shorea* and *Dipterocarpus* species, mingled with oaks, *Tristaniopsis burmanica*, *Anneslea fragrans*, *Craibiodendron stellatum*, and so on. At the onset of the hot dry season, these trees produce a flaming red or orange canopy before they to drop their leaves in response to declining soil moisture. Many tree species flower when leafless, supposedly to make their flowers more visible to prospective pollinators. Flowering epiphytic orchids add colour to the canopy at the same time.

Deciduous dipterocarp-oak forest supports a wide range of birds, including Scarlet-backed Flowerpecker, Little Pied Flycatcher, Lineated Barbet and at least six different species of bulbul. Buzzards and other raptors commonly soar overhead, seeking prey such as Indochinese Ground Squirrels.

One of the most interesting mammals in this habitat is the Burmese Ferret-badger, still quite common on Doi Suthep. This nocturnal mammal has the black-and-white coloration of a badger with a body shape similar to that of a ferret. When threatened, it defends itself like a skunk, by spraying a foetid secretion from a gland near its anus into the face of its approaching enemy.

Left: *Plants of the ginger family are very common in the ground flora of the forest on Doi Suthep. This Hedychium species is only one of at least 46 ginger species recorded on the mountain.*

Below: *Ferns and mosses provide permanent splashes of green around Doi Suthep's many waterfalls.*

Mixed Deciduous Forest

Mixed deciduous forest, characterized by enormous *Dipterocarpus costatus* trees, which look like gigantic sticks of broccoli, begins to occur at an elevation of approximately 700 metres (2,300 feet). The trees are generally taller – up to 30 metres (98 feet) – than those of deciduous dipterocarp-oak forest, and the canopy is more-or-less closed. Many trees in this forest have beautiful flowers, which are particularly abundant in the late dry season (e.g. *Bauhinia variegata*, *Metadina trichotoma*). Amongst the ground flora, the aroid *Amorphophallus sootepensis* is one of more than 500 plant species named from specimens first collected on Doi Suthep, making the park of crucial significance to the science of plant taxonomy in Thailand.

Evergreen Forest

At an elevation of approximately 1,000 metres (3,281 feet), evergreen forest begins to dominate. On Doi Suthep this contains a very wide range of tree species. Beneath the dense canopy, light is in short supply and some plants have evolved the means to do without it. Parasitic plants such as *Balanophora* (four species on Doi Suthep) and the striking, red *Sapria himalayana*

Right: *The famous temple, Wat Pratat attracts more than a million visitors to Doi Suthep every year. It is one of the most sacred sites for Buddhists in Thailand.*

Below: *A monk 'ordains' a tree by wrapping a robe around it. Trees often have high spiritual significance in Thai culture, and are believed to house spirits, both good and evil.*

extract nutriment from the roots of other plants, whilst delicate herbs such as *Hypopithys lanuginosa* feed on decomposing organic matter.

Doi Suthep's evergreen forest provides an important stopover for birds during their annual migrations. Common winter visitors include Grey Nightjar, Slender-billed Oriole and Orange-flanked Bush-robin (known in Europe as Red-flanked Bluetail). Some of Doi Suthep's more colourful evergreen forest residents include iridescent green pigeons, barbets and leafbirds, orange or yellow minivets and blue flycatchers and pittas.

Birds are not the only flying animals in the evergreen forest on Doi Suthep. Tiny grey squirrels avoid predators on the ground by gliding between trees using membranes stretched between their fore and hind legs. Flying lizards also occur. The upper slopes are also home to at least seven non-flying squirrel species and it is a last refuge for Doi Suthep's remaining larger mammals, including Common Palm Civet, Leopard Cat, Bush-tailed Porcupine and Common Barking Deer.

Forest Restoration

Like many of Thailand's national parks, Doi Suthep has suffered considerably from deforestation. Various estimates of forest cover range from only 40 per cent up to 70 per cent of the park. To help solve the problem of deforestation, one project is developing ways to restore forest to degraded areas. The Forest Restoration Research Unit (FORRU) is a joint initiative between the national park authority and Chiang Mai University's (CMU) Department of Biology. At an experimental tree nursery near the national park headquarters, FORRU staff and CMU students have developed new methods to propagate a wide range of forest tree species indigenous to the park. So far, more than 400 species have been germinated from seed and grown in the nursery. FORRU also helped to establish a community tree nursery at one of the Hmong villages in the national park, Ban Mae Sa Mai, where the feasibility of new tree-propagation methods developed by the project are tested by local people. In experimental plots near the village, FORRU is testing the suitability of the framework species method of forest restoration by planting mixtures of up to 30 tree species, capable of rapidly shading out weeds and attracting wildlife. Previously blamed for forest destruction, hill-tribe villagers in the park now join in tree-planting events and protect the planted trees from forest fire. With changing attitudes and greater scientific knowledge, the forest and its wildlife are slowly returning.

Spiritual Significance

In addition to its ecological value, Doi Suthep is of great spiritual significance to Chiang Mai's inhabitants. Doi Suthep's cultural history stretches much farther back than the founding of Wat Pratat. The Guardian Spirits of Chiang Mai reside on the mountain's lower slopes. Every year these spirits are placated in a ceremony that has its origins in myths that stretch back more than 1,000 years. The ceremony involves the sacrificial slaughter of a young buffalo, to satisfy the spirits' lust for meat. A medium then becomes possessed with the spirits and eats the raw buffalo carcass.

Right: *Folded hills disappear into the haze. A typical view of the northern highlands.*

Below: *The Leopard Cat, one of a few large mammals still surviving on Doi Suthep, is more tolerant of human disturbance than any other wild cat species, and is often found around villages.*

KHLONG LAN NATIONAL PARK

Wonderful Waterfalls

Waterfalls, rapids and magnificent riverine scenery are the main attractions at Khlong Lan National Park, but the area is also a strategic part of the Western Forest Complex, forming part of the northeastern boundary of the largest conservation area in Southeast Asia. Covering an area of 300 square kilometres (116 square miles), Khlong Lan National Park was established in 1982 to protect the last remaining forest in the northern province of Kamphaeng Phet.

Opposite, left above:
Forest in reasonably good condition covers about 60 percent of the park.

Opposite, left centre: *The rare Impressed Tortoise feeds mainly on mushrooms.*

Opposite, left below: *A few White-handed Gibbons still sing in the more remote areas of the park.*

Opposite, right: *Waterfalls are the main attraction at Khlong Lan. They feed into the Chao Phraya River, a vital water supply for agriculture and urban development.*

Above, right: *An Akha woman with traditional silver head gear goes to work.*

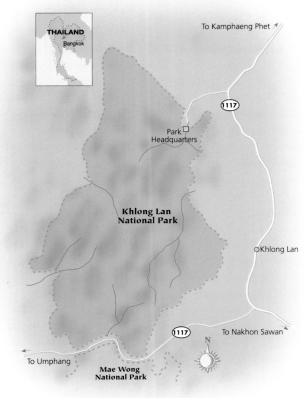

The Importance of Water

One of the main reasons for creating this national park was its importance as a water-catchment area. Khlong Lan's forested mountains, rising to a maximum elevation of 1,439 metres (4,721 feet) at Khun Khlong Lan, form part of the Thanon Thongchai mountain range. They encompass the headwaters of several major tributaries (particularly the Khlong Klung and Khlong Suan Mark) of the Ping River, which flows into the Chao Phraya River, supplying water to irrigate the rice fields of the Central Plains and supply urban and industrial development around Bangkok.

The Attraction of Water

Water is also the main tourist attraction in the park. The recreational value of Khlong Lan Waterfall, near the park headquarters, has long been recognized by government officials. Above the falls, five streams, draining Khun Khlong Lan mountain, converge in a small lake on a plateau. From there, their combined flow is funnelled down a narrow gully for 3 kilometres (2 miles), before plummeting 100 metres (328 feet) down a dramatic cliff face, 40 metres (131 feet) wide, into a placid pool, ideal

Location: Kamphaeng Phet Province, approximately 50 km (31 miles) southwest of the provincial capital.

Climate: Monsoonal; average annual temperature 23°C (73°F); average annual rainfall approximately 978 mm (39 in); rainy season May–October; cool, dry season November–January; hot, dry season February–April.

When to Go: End of the rainy season is best for the waterfalls.

Access: By road, from Bangkok, travel north on Highway 32 to Nakorn Sawan and Highway 1 to Kamphaeng Phet. At Km 346, turn west at Ban Klong Mae Lai Market (Highway 1117). After 46 km (29 miles), turn west at Klong Lan Market, 4 km (2½ miles) to the park headquarters. Public buses depart from Bangkok's northern bus terminal to Kamphaeng Phet, from where local transport can be hired to the park headquarters.

Permits: None required. Entrance fees charged at the waterfalls.

Equipment: Insect repellent; light clothes and boots for forest walks; swimming gear.

Facilities: Seven bungalows, accommodating 5 to 12 people each, for rent; campsites; restaurants at the falls; small visitor centre with exhibition at the park headquarters.

Watching Wildlife: Small mammals; 84 bird species.

Visitor Activities: Forest walks; visiting waterfalls.

Above: *Despite earlier logging and occupation of the area by hill tribes, Khlong Lan still retains extensive forests well worth exploring.*

In former times, such forest had abundant wildlife, such as Asian Elephant, Gaur, Banteng and Tiger, all sadly now extirpated by hunting. Smaller mammals, such as Common Barking Deer, Common Wild Pig, various squirrels, a few monkeys and White-handed Gibbons, do, however, remain.

A total of 84 bird species have been confirmed within the park, mostly common woodland species, the more species-rich groups being leafbirds, babblers, warblers, bulbuls and flycatchers. Mahidol University's Conservation Data Centre lists 34 species of reptile and 25 amphibians as confirmed within the national park, including the endangered Burmese Horned Toad.

Difficult Decisions

Before being declared a national park, Khlong Lan had been inhabited by Communist rebels. In addition, settlements of several hill tribes, such as the Hmong, Yao, Lahu, Akha and Lisu, had a significant impact on the national park. At first, the hill-tribe communities were allowed to stay, but their agricultural activities were rapidly destroying the integrity of the watershed. Hill-tribe agriculture involves felling forest, cultivating the land for a few years and then allowing forest to re-invade the abandoned fields to replenish the soil. The system works well where population density is low, but at Khlong Lan migration of large numbers of hill-tribe people into the area meant that such cultivation methods could be practised only at the expense of the forest. Hunting of wildlife and growing of opium poppies were additional problems. In 1986, therefore, the hill-tribe villages were relocated outside the boundaries of the park.

for swimming. This impressive spectacle draws thousands of visitors every year. Inevitably the area around the falls has been developed to meet their needs. A large carpark, picnic sites and stalls, selling food and souvenirs, create an unsightly distraction from the natural beauty of the falls.

Also worth a visit are Khlong Nam Lai Waterfalls, also known as Pang Kwai, approximately 25 kilometres (16 miles) from the park headquarters along Highway 1117, via a turn off near Khlong Lan sub-district. The falls descend over nine tiers, with a swimming pool near the third tier. One of the attractions of these falls is the deep black colour of the rocks.

At Kaeng Kao Roi, rapids, sandy beaches and thousand of tiny rocks, set against a magnificent scenic backdrop, provide a quieter attraction, away from the crowds around the falls.

Forests and Wildlife

Right: *Akha hill-tribe mothers traditionally carry young children on their backs. At Khlong Lan, hill-tribe settlements have been relocated outside the park boundary to prevent further forest destruction.*

Despite the damage caused by loggers and hill tribes in the past, Khlong Lan still retains expansive areas of bamboo deciduous and evergreen forests, in good condition. In bamboo deciduous forest the common trees include various species of *Shorea*, *Lagerstroemia* and *Terminalia*, *Pterocarpus macrocarpus*, *Afzelia xylocarpa* and the occasional teak tree. In evergreen forest, fine specimens of *Schima wallichii*, *Manglietia garrettii*, *Phoebe lanceolata* and *Garcinia* have escaped the chainsaws.

MAE PING NATIONAL PARK

A River Voyage through Limestone Cliffs

Before completion of the railway in 1921, travellers between Bangkok and the northern capital, Chiang Mai, made the journey by river. An arduous trip, lasting from six weeks to three months, small boats were propelled up the Chao Phraya and Ping Rivers with oars and long poles spiked with iron. Especially hazardous were rapids approximately 120 kilometres (75 miles) south of Chiang Mai. The late 19th-century traveller Carl Brock described this stretch of river thus: ...'the banks of the river are hemmed in with limestone mountains, which stand out like silhouettes against the bright blue sky, studded to the top with trees and vegetation growing in a bewildering but enchanting confusion. The whole face of the cliffs was alive with bats and swallows, flitting about their nests, scooped out in the soft stone.'

Although the rapids are now drowned beneath water held back by the huge

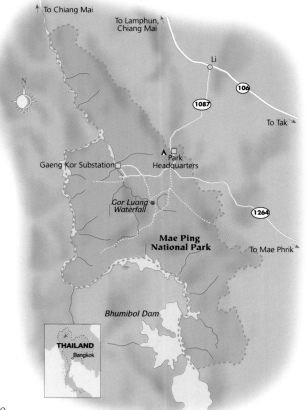

Bhumibol Dam, the majestic cliffs remain and the sense of awe of those intrepid early travellers can still be experienced by visiting Mae Ping National Park.

Boats to the Park

Boat trips into the national park begin at Doi Tao Reservoir south of Chiang Mai. The journey downstream takes about two hours. Approaching the park from the south, boats may be chartered at Sam Ngao, to travel upstream 65 kilometres (41 miles), taking five or six hours to reach the park. The main river access point in the park is Gaeng Kor substation, approximately 20 kilometres (12 miles) west of the park headquarters. There, floating accommodation and short boat trips up or down the river to view extraordinary limestone formations, caves, waterfalls and a sunken temple can be arranged. Along the river, kingfishers, swallows and Long-tailed Macaques can be seen. Bats are abundant, sweeping the air above the river for insects and roosting in vast numbers in the many caves that riddle the park. In former times, villagers collected bat dung to make gunpowder.

Above, right: The Leopard Cat is one of the most widespread of Asia's cat species.

Location: In the provinces of Chiang Mai, Lampoon and Tak, 120 km (75 miles) south of Chiang Mai City.

Climate: Monsoonal, mean annual rainfall about 700 mm (28 in); wettest in May, driest in December and January; rainy season May–October; cool season November–January (minimum temperature 14°C/57°F); hot dry season February–April (maximum temperature 38°C/100°F).

When to Go: Avoid the rainy season, when road access is difficult.

Access: By boat, two hours downstream from Doi Tao or six hours upstream from Sam Ngao. By car, follow Highway 106 south from Chiang Mai to Li, turn west on Highway 1087, 20 km (12 miles) to the park headquarters. No public transport.

Permits: None required. Telephone the park (053) 519031 to arrange your visit.

Equipment: Protection against malaria; light clothes and tough shoes for forest walks; warm clothes for the cool season and waterproofs during the rainy season; swimming gear; a torch for caves.

Facilities: At the park headquarters, a small visitor centre and campsite; a floating dormitory and campsite at Gaeng Kor substation; boats for hire.

Watching Wildlife: Deer, wild pigs, monkeys; at least 73 bird species.

Visitor Activities: Boat trips on the river; visiting waterfalls and caves; birdwatching.

Superb Deciduous Forests

Mae Ping National Park, totalling 1,003 square kilometres (387 square miles), was created in 1981 to protect the alluvial flood plain of the Ping River and surrounding hills, which are a vital watershed area for the Bhumibol Dam. The park supports some of the finest stretches of deciduous dipterocarp forest in the country. In most other areas, deciduous dipterocarp forest trees rarely exceed 15 metres (50 feet) in height, and birds are scarce. In Mae Ping National Park, however, many of the *Dipterocarpus obtusifolius* trees reach 25 metres (82 feet), and the forest is alive with birds such as woodpeckers, bulbuls, laughingthrushes, drongos and parakeets.

Waterfall in Teak Forest

Near Gor Luang Waterfall, the park retains a tiny remnant of the original teak forest that once covered most of northern Thailand. Teak forests were almost entirely destroyed, mostly by foreign logging companies, in the late 19th and early 20th centuries, completely changing the character of northern Thailand's vegetation. But around Gor Luang Waterfall huge teak trees somehow escaped the loggers, along with other tree species typical of teak forest (e.g. *Xylia xylocarpa, Afzelia xylocarpa, Dalbergia cultrata, Pterocarpus macrocarpus* and *Lagerstroemia cochinchinensis*). The waterfalls are exquisitely beautiful. Sheets of water glide over limestone curtains into an aquamarine pool.

Above: *With its greatly elongated tail and deep orange underparts, the White-rumped Shama is unmistakable, as is its rich and melodious song.*

Right: *McClelland's Coral Snake hunts other snakes and lizards at night on the forest floor, in lowland forests up to 1,000 m elevation.*

Unusual Meadows

The extraordinary vegetation of Thung Gig, in the east of the park, is well worth a visit. There, deciduous dipterocarp forest gradually gives way to open grassland, studded with fire-resistant *Phoenix* palms and frequented by Siamese Hare, Common Wild Pig and Common Barking Deer. Huge numbers of Grey-headed Parakeets roost in this area at dusk, filling the air with their shrill whistling calls. An underlying basin of impervious rock, covered by waterlogged, peaty soil, makes it impossible for trees to grow there.

Wildlife

The Malay Pangolin and the Slow Loris are still common in the park, the latter stalking insects and searching for fruit in the forest canopy at night. Serows haunt the limestone cliffs. The park supports a diverse range of reptiles. Elongated Tortoises trundle through deciduous forest, feeding on shoots, fruits and mushrooms, whilst flying lizards glide between the trees. In streams and rivers, soft-shelled turtles search for water snails. Visitors should beware of poisonous snakes, such as Blue Krait and White-lipped Pit-viper, whose bites can be fatal.

The park supports at least 73 bird species; a checklist is available from the park headquarters. White-rumped Falcon, Crested Serpent Eagle and Black Baza are among the birds of prey, whilst waterfowl include Grey Heron, Red-wattled Lapwing and Cinnamon Bittern.

Above: *After removal of teak trees by logging, the forest often becomes dominated by tall bamboos. Near Gor Luang Waterfalls a few of the original teak trees can still be seen.*

Far left: *The beautiful waterfalls of Gor Luang, one of many tributaries of the Mae Ping.*

Left: Aeginetia indica *is a common parasitic plant found in deciduous forests. It flowers in November..*

MAE WONG NATIONAL PARK

Teak Forest on the Road to Recovery

Until about 120 years ago, teak was the dominant tree species in northern Thailand's lowland forests. Towards the end of the 19th century, however, coercion from potential colonial powers allowed foreign companies to plunder Thailand's teak forests, transforming them into secondary growth. At Mae Wong National Park, however, it is possible to imagine what the original teak forests were like. Although the park was extensively logged, several areas retain abundant teak, making Mae Wong one of the two most important sites for conservation of this valuable tree in Thailand (the other being Mae Yom National Park).

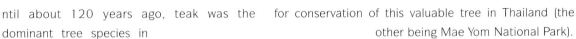

Covering 894 square kilometres (345 square miles) of the Thanon Thongchai mountain range, Mae Wong National Park protects watersheds of crucial tributaries of the Ping River. It adjoins the much larger wildlife sanctuaries of Huay Kha Khaeng (to the south) and Umphang (to the west) and is therefore vital to the integrity of the Western Forest Complex. The park is bisected west to east by the Wong River valley, after which it is named. The area was first suggested as a national park in 1983, but it was not formally declared until 1987, after hill-tribe communities were forcibly removed. Mae Wong is now one of very few national parks that does not contain settlements.

Teak Forest

Regenerating teak forest, with up to 7,500 teak trees per square kilometre (19,430 per square mile), occurs patchily throughout the park. Teak can be recognized from its pale brown bark with closely spaced longitudinal furrows, large round leaves and yellowish-white clusters of flowers, which speckle the forest canopy

Opposite, above: *A wide variety of forest habitats can be seen at Mae Wong, from tall dense forest in almost pristine condition, to logged-over secondary forest in the process of recovery.*

Opposite, below left: *Preferring more open areas of woodland, the Hoopoe is named after the sound of its call, a soft* hoop-hoop-hoop.

Opposite, below right: *Figs provide a vital supply of food for wildlife throughout the year.*

Above, right: *A Syntomid moth with transparent wings active by day.*

Location: In the provinces of Kamphaeng Phet and Nakhon Sawan, approximately 75 km (47 miles) southeast of Kamphaeng Phet City.

Climate: Monsoonal; mean annual rainfall 1,100 mm (43 in); rainy season May–October; cool, dry season November–January (minimum temperature down to 2°C/36°F); hot, dry season February–April (maximum temperature up to 43°C/109°F).

When to Go: Cool season is best for forest hikes.

Access: By car 386 km (241 miles) from Bangkok, travel north along Highway 1 through Nakhon Sawan. About 50 km (31 miles) before Kamphaeng Phet, at Khlong Khlung, turn west on Highway 1242, 60 km (37 miles) to the park headquarters.

Permits: None required. Telephone the park headquarters at 055 719010–1 to arrange your visit.

Equipment: Insect repellent; hiking boots and light clothes for forest treks; warm clothes for the cool season; waterproofs.

Facilities: Bungalows for rent and camping at the park headquarters and Chong Yen; camping also at Mae Rewa; food available only at the headquarters; nature trails; long-distance trails with guides.

Watching Wildlife: Mostly small mammals; deer, squirrels, and so on; a wide diversity of birds, including hornbills.

Visitor Activities: Forest walks; birdwatching; visiting waterfalls and a scenic drive.

Above: *Sunset over one of the more degraded areas of Mae Wong's varied forest habitats.*

Above, right: *The Oriental Pied Hornbill is the most common hornbill species in Thailand. It is more resistant to forest disturbance than other hornbills, and plays an important role in forest regeneration by dispersing seeds.*

from August to October. In addition to the teak itself, the forest also contains other valuable timber species including *Afzelia xylocarpa*, *Xylia xylocarpa*, *Pterocarpus macrocarpus* and several species of *Shorea*, whilst in more disturbed areas, bamboo predominates. The teak forests provide a home for several rare bird species, including Yellow-footed Pigeon and Yellow-crowned Woodpecker, and one of the most significant populations of the Alexandrine Parakeet.

Wildlife

The fauna of the park is known to include 57 mammal species, 305 birds, 22 reptiles and 7 amphibians, but surveys are far from complete. Easily seen birds include flycatchers, minivets, barbets, bulbuls, Red Junglefowl, Hoopoe and nightjars. Although a few Asian Elephants and Gaurs occasionally migrate into the park from surrounding areas, they are rarely seen. Tigers and Leopards have recently been recorded, but are probably very rare. Banteng, Malayan Tapir and Serow may be commoner. Smaller, more easily seen mammals include squirrels, civets, martens, porcupines and otters.

Scenic Road

The Khlong Lan to Umphang road along the northern boundary of the park offers excellent views over the forest and access to the park headquarters (Km 65). Near the headquarters are the popular tourist attractions of Kang Pha Koy Nang rapids and Pha Koy Nang Waterfall; the latter leaps over a granite cliff in four huge steps.

The Chong Yen substation at Km 93 is surrounded by evergreen forest. A cool breeze is funnelled between two mountains; at an elevation of 1,340 metres (4,396 feet), the average temperature is below 20°C (68°F). The forest there is brimming with epiphytic ferns and orchids, whilst tree ferns create a primeval atmosphere. On the forest floor, parasitic *Sapria himlayana* flowers emerge through the leaf litter. Chong Yen is a good place to look for hornbills: four species (Wreathed, Rufous-necked, Great and Oriental Pied) live in the park. Beyond Chong Yen, the road is closed to traffic, creating a quiet trail for birdwatchers. The serenity of this trail is, however, threatened by plans to renovate the road all the way to Umphang.

A wide range of long-distance hikes can be arranged with guides from the national park. From Chong Yen, a full day's trek leads to Nang Nuan Waterfall, whilst a round trip to the park's highest point, Mo Kochoo mountain ridge (1,960 metres/6,430 feet), takes five to seven days. For the less adventurous, three self-guided nature trails meander around the park headquarters, showcasing the wildlife of teak and bamboo deciduous forest.

Threats to the Forest

Although Mae Wong's forest appears to be recovering, constant vigilance by the park authorities will be necessary if the forests are to make a full recovery. Valuable timber trees are an irresistible attraction to illegal loggers. Corrupt businessmen and officials easily exploit impoverished villagers to cut the trees. Hunting remains a serious problem, having all but eliminated the largest mammal species. A plan to build a dam on the Wong River threatens the park's ecological integrity.

Nam Tok Mae Surin National Park

Thailand's Tallest Waterfall

Spectacular views over misty valleys, hill-tribe villages and one of Thailand's most impressive waterfalls (*nam tok* in Thai) are the main attractions of this far-northern park. Created in 1981, Nam Tok Mae Surin National Park covers 397 square kilometres (153 square miles) of rolling hills and ravines in the Thanon Thongchai mountain range, rising to a maximum elevation of 1,752 metres (5,748 feet). The park is long and narrow in shape – barely 12 kilometres (7½ miles) wide – with a north–south orientation, located along the eastern side of the main road between Mae Hong Son and Mae Sariang (Highway 108), just a few kilometres from the international border with Myanmar.

The park headquarters lies a few kilometres to the northeast of the sleepy town of Mae Hong Son, dubbed 'Thailand's Shangri-La', with its Burmese-style temples and traditional market. Around the headquarters, a small zoo and arboretum showcases local trees and indigenous animals rescued from the illegal wildlife trade. Nearby, the banks of the River Pai provide a tranquil setting for

Above, right: *The Ashy Drongo prefers evergreen and mixed evergreen deciduous forest. The species breeds in northwestern Thailand from March to August, constructing a shallow, cup-shaped nest, suspended from a tree branch.*

picnics and swimming. Voyages downstream on flimsy bamboo rafts can be arranged for the adventurous. The conservation value of the park is enhanced by it being contiguous with Lum Nam Pai Wildlife Sanctuary to the north.

The Waterfall

The main scenic attraction is Mae Surin Waterfall, which lies in the extreme southeastern part of the park. From the park headquarters and Mae Hong Son City, visitors must travel south on Highway 108, turning east at Khun Yuam on Highway 1263. It is probably Thailand's tallest single-tier waterfall. A single jet of water plunges over a sheer cliff, falling 80 metres (262 feet) in a single step, crashing onto a jumble of boulders below, with a rainbow arching through the spray. The spectacular falls can be seen from a viewpoint across the valley or approached on foot. Some of the pools downstream from the falls are suitable for swimming.

Hill Tribes

The route to Mae Surin Waterfall takes visitors through several Hmong and Karen hill-tribe villages. Northern Thailand is the adopted home of at least 10 ethnic minorities who prefer to establish their settlements in upland areas. The Hmong originated in southern China and Laos. Traditionally occupying areas above an elevation of 1,000 metres (3,281 feet), their economy used

Location: In Mae Hong Son Province, a few km east and south of the provincial capital.

Climate: Monsoonal; mean annual rainfall 1,230 mm (48 in); mean annual temperature 26°C (79°F); rainy season June–September; cool season October–February (minimum temperature 12°C/54°F); hot season March–May (maximum temperature 39°C/102°F).

When to Go: The cool season is the most comfortable time of year for forest walks and provides the best opportunity for observing winter migrant birds.

Access: Mae Hong Son is accessible by air, road or public bus from Chiang Mai. Park visitors should rent a four-wheel-drive vehicle in Mae Hong Son or book a tour at one of the many travel agencies in the city.

Permits: None required. Entrance fees are charged at the waterfalls.

Equipment: Insect repellent; protection against malaria; light clothes and strong shoes for forest walks; warm clothes essential at night; waterproof gear; swimming gear.

Facilities: Bungalows for rent at the park headquarters; campsites at the park headquarters and at Mae Surin Waterfall; visitors must bring their own food; nature trail.

Watching Wildlife: Gibbons, wild pigs, deer, Serows; bulbuls, woodpeckers, warblers, drongos, and so on.

Visitor Activities: Forest walks; visiting waterfalls; bird-watching; swimming, and rafting trips along the Pai River.

Above: *In degraded deciduous forest, bamboos shade out the germinating seeds of trees. Vines and lianas proliferate, often smothering isolated trees and competing with them for light, soil moisture and nutrients.*

to rely heavily on the growing of opium, but now alternative upland crops are grown including cabbages, corn, upland rice and lychees. Such crops do, however, require a much larger land area than opium to make a reasonable living, resulting in increased deforestation. Mostly originating from Myanmar, the Karen usually live at lower altitudes than the Hmong, and their methods of agriculture are regarded as more environmentally friendly. A wide range of crops is grown in mixed home gardens that retain a lot of forest cover.

A Golden Killer

Another major tourist attraction en route to Mae Surin Waterfalls is the famous Thung Bua Thong, or field of golden lotus flowers. In November, when they flower, these plants turn the hillsides into a mass of glorious yellow. Despite its beauty, however, this species, the Mexican Sunflower, is a rapacious exotic weed and creates a serious ecological problem. Invasive and persistent, the plant smothers the native flora and hinders forest regeneration on denuded hillsides. Since, however, the spectacle of golden flowers draws many tourists to Mae Hong

Son Province, appeals from ecologists for its removal or control will continue to fall on deaf ears.

Wildlife

The park supports deciduous dipterocarp forest and bamboo deciduous forest at lower elevations with evergreen forest higher up. Most of the forest in the national park is, however, degraded, which, along with heavy hunting pressure, makes wildlife rather scarce. A few scattered teak trees remain amongst the bamboo, and there are some fine stands of pine at higher elevations. Recently reported mammals in the national park include Malayan Sun Bear, Serow, Common Wild Pig, Golden Cat, Common Barking Deer and several species of squirrel and civet. The songs of gibbons can still be heard in the remotest areas of the park.

The low number of bird species recorded in the park (46) probably reflects the lack of a thorough survey rather than actual low species diversity. Confirmed birds include White-rumped Falcon, Asian Barred Owlet, Oriental Pied Hornbill, Black-headed Woodpecker and several species of bulbul, drongo, warbler and flycatcher.

Above, left: *Protected leaf buds and a deep root system help this young sapling of* Dipterocarpus tuberculatus *to withstand frequent fires and drought.*

Above, right: *Wat Chong Kham is one of several Burmese-style temples in Mae Hong Son town.*

Left: *Common Barking Deer is one of the last large mammal species to disappear when forests are disturbed. Their barks are often heard at night but they are rarely seen.*

Nam Nao National Park

Elephants and Pine Trees

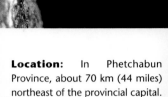

Easy forest walks and chances to see Asian Elephants and other large mammals in the unlikely setting of pine forest are the main attractions of this superb national park. Declared in 1972, Nam Nao National Park covers a total area of 990 square kilometres (386 square miles), but the value of the park is enormously enhanced by it being contiguous with the much larger Phu Kiew Wildlife Sanctuary to the south. In combination, the park and sanctuary protect a total of 2,550 square kilometres (984 square miles) of sandstone hills in the Phetchabun Range, mostly covered in deciduous dipterocarp forest and pine-dipterocarp forest, with narrow strips of evergreen forest bordering streams and rivers. The highest point in the park, the summit of Phu Phaa Jit, is at 1,271 metres (4,170 feet) above sea level.

Pine-dipterocarp Forest

South of the national park headquarters and the main highway, an extensive network of tracks and trails meanders through one of the most extensive areas of open pine-dipterocarp forest in Thailand. Massive, three-needled pine trees (*Pinus kesiya*) tower above typical deciduous dipterocarp forest trees, which include several species of *Dipterocarpus*, *Shorea*, *Quercus* and *Dalbergia*, as well as *Ochna integerrima*, *Buchanania lanzan*, *Craibiodendron stellatum* and *Gluta usitata*.

Grasses and sedges dominate the ground flora, with splashes of colour provided by pink or white *Curcuma* species, yellow *Globba obscura* and the fragile pink orchid, *Arundina graminifolia*. *Aeginetia pedunculata* is a parasite on the roots of grasses. Its stalkless, purple-and-yellow, trumpet-shaped flowers appear just above the soil surface, particularly where fire has recently cleared away the surrounding vegetation. Also associated with pine trees is the curiously shaped fungus,

Map labels: Nam Nao National Park; THAILAND Bangkok; Pha Hong; Park Headquarters; 12; Ban Peak; Sai Ngun Waterfall; Sai Thong Waterfall; Heo Sai Waterfall; Phu Phaa Jit 1271m (4170ft); Suan Son; Chulabhorn Reservoir

Opposite, above: *Nam Nao National Park retains a small population of Asian Elephants, most easily seen lumbering through pine forests south of the park headquarters.*

Opposite, below left: *The Black-throated Laughingthrush is a common resident of Nam Nao National Park.*

Opposite, below centre: *Several caves within the park contain impressive formations. They are home to hundreds of thousands of bats.*

Opposite, below right: *Flowering orchids attract plant enthusiasts to Nam Nao's deciduous forest late in the dry season.*

Above, right: *Thaumantis diores sips rainwater running down a tree trunk.*

Location: In Phetchabun Province, about 70 km (44 miles) northeast of the provincial capital.

Climate: Monsoonal, mean temperature 27°C (81°F), mean annual rainfall about 1,180 mm (46 in); rainy season May–September (15–20 rainy days per month); cool season November–February (minimum temperature 2°C/36°F); hot dry season February–April (maximum temperature 35°C/95°F).

When to Go: The early rainy season is the best time to see large animals.

Access: By road along Highway 12, west from Khon Kaen or east from Phitsanulok and Lomsak. The road bisects the park between kilometre stones 28 and 72. Bus services running along Highway 12 can be requested to stop very close to the park headquarters.

Permits: An entrance fee is charged.

Equipment: Warm clothes for evenings; light clothes and tough shoes for walking; a spotlight for viewing wildlife at night.

Facilities: Bungalows, providing accommodation for eight to 50 people, for rent at the park headquarters, and campsites; a restaurant and small exhibition at the park headquarters; an extensive network of short nature trails and long-distance footpaths.

Watching Wildlife: Asian Elephants, deer, wild cattle and primates; more than 250 bird species.

Visitor Activities: Forest walks; watching wildlife.

Macrolepida procera. The immature mushroom looks like a fluffy golf ball on the end of a thick, brown stalk, before the cap expands to the size of a dinner plate.

Large Mammals

Fires sweep across this area annually, but the sweet young grass, which shoots up afterwards, provides irresistible grazing for Banteng, Gaur, Sambar Deer, Common Barking Deer and Fea's Barking Deer. The latter, recognized by the IUCN as an endangered species, is mostly confined to the west of central Thailand and adjoining areas of Myanmar. It is distinguished from the Common Barking Deer by having a black dorsal surface to its tail (as opposed to brown on the Common Barking Deer). It is the Asian Elephants, however, that are the star attractions of this savannah-like area.

Approximately 100 are estimated to reside in the park. Being a semi-open habitat, it is probably easier to see elephants here during the daytime than it is at Khao Yai. Lumbering through the pine trees in small herds, they create an almost surrealistic vision.

National park staff have created a series of small ponds and salt licks scattered across this area, which act like a magnet for wildlife, especially during the evenings. Wildlife watchers keeping vigil at these spots at dawn or dusk will rarely be disappointed. The pools and salt licks draw not only herbivores and wildlife enthusiasts, however: there are also an estimated 20 to 50 Tigers in the park that doubtless stalk prey attracted by the water and minerals. In addition to Tigers, Clouded Leopard and the elusive and highly endangered Marbled Cat have been recorded.

Below: *Sambar are Thailand's largest deer species. They require large amounts of calcium to replace their antlers each year and can often be seen at mineral licks.*

Other Wildlife

Nam Nao and Phu Kiew were probably the last strongholds of the Sumatran Rhino and Eld's Deer in Thailand, but it is very unlikely that either of these two species still exists in the wild. Plenty of other species are, however, still present in the park, including three species of macaque monkey (Pig-tailed, Long-tailed and Stump-tailed) and White-handed Gibbons. Both bear species (Asiatic Black and Malayan Sun), as well as Asian Wild Dog, Yellow-throated Marten and Crestless Himalayan Porcupine, are reportedly present.

One of the best places for watching birds is along the network of short nature trails around the park headquarters, which showcase the full range of forest types within the park. Confirmed bird species for Nam Nao number 252. Notable species include Mountain Hawk Eagle, Eurasian Hobby, Silver Pheasant, Coral-billed Ground Cuckoo, Rufous-tailed Robin, Siberian Rubythroat and Verditer Flycatcher.

The park also has quite a reputation amongst butterfly enthusiasts. Some of the more colourful species include Common Birdwing, Paris Peacock, Banded Swallowtail, Common Blue Bottle, Red Lacewing, Lurcher and Great Nawab.

Left: *With its dense heads of greenish-yellow flowers and thorny stems,* Trevesia palmata *is unmistakable. It is a small tree found in the understorey of evergreen forests.*

Above: *The Verditer Flycatcher can be seen swooping on flying insects from exposed perches, especially along the edge of the forest.*

Left: *The Green Pit-viper stalks its prey in the forest canopy at night. It is a highly poisonous snake and should be given a wide berth if seen.*

OB LUANG NATIONAL PARK

'Grand Canyon' and Prehistoric Paintings

Established in 1991, Ob Luang National Park protects 553 square kilometres (213 square miles) of steep, forested, granite hills, adjoining the much higher mountains of Doi Inthanon National Park to the northwest. Ranging in elevation from 200 metres (656 feet), along the Mae Chaem River, to 1,656 metres (5,433 feet), in the northeast, the park forms the watershed of the Mae Chaem River, a major tributary of the Ping River. This river rushes through the dramatic Ob Luang Gorge, the park's central feature, a narrow ravine with sheer sides and a raging torrent at the bottom. The main reason for visiting Ob Luang, however, is the informative nature trail near the park headquarters, which offers a succinct introduction to the use of northern Thailand's forest by human beings from the Stone Age to the present day, as well as vertigo-inducing views of the gorge.

Opposite, left above: *The Serow is a black goat-like antelope, which inhabits densely forested steep cliffs and mountains.*

Opposite, left centre: *The Goral is a rare goat-like antelope restricted in Thailand to Mountains west of the Ping River.*

Opposite, left below: *A Changeable Hawk Eagle looks for prey.*

Opposite, right: *A flimsy bridge crosses the gorge at Ob Luang.*

Above, right: *A Blue-throated Barbet.*

Welcome to the Stone Age

Approximately 4,000–5,000 years ago, a group of hunter-gatherers, now called Hoabinhians by archaeologists, camped under a rocky overhang on the side of a narrow valley filled with dense tropical rainforest and teeming with wildlife. Every year, migrating animals became concentrated in this valley as they passed between their rainy-season and dry-season feeding grounds, providing excellent hunting for these Stone Age people. Sitting under the rock shelter, they fashioned crude wooden weapons using unpolished stone-flaked axes. After a successful kill, stone tools were also used to butcher the carcasses, before bringing the meat back to the shelter, probably for cooking over open fires. With such an abundant supply of food, these people had enough leisure time to depict their hunting activities in red and white paint on the cliff wall. The faint and fragmented remains of these paintings can still be seen today.

Later, during the Bronze Age, a different race of people established permanent settlements nearby, leaving behind signs of a more-advanced civilization: bronze tools, jewelry and pottery. A gravesite from this period, with an explanatory plaque, can be seen on the nature trail. The Bronze Age was probably the first period in

---

Location: Chiang Mai Province, approximately 85 km (53 miles) southwest of the provincial capital.

Climate: Monsoonal; mean annual temperature 26°C (79°F); mean annual rainfall 915 mm (36 in); rainy season May–October; cool, dry season November–February; hot, dry season April–May.

When to Go: The cool season provides comfortable temperatures for walking and the greatest diversity of birds.

Access: By car from Chiang Mai, travel south to Hot, then 19 km (12 miles) west on Highway 108 to the park headquarters. Public buses from Chiang Mai to Mae Sariang can be asked to stop at the park headquarters.

Permits: Entrance fees are charged.

Equipment: Light clothes, boots for forest walks.

Facilities: At the park headquarters, bungalows for rent; campsite; restaurant; archaeological exhibition; nature trail.

Watching Wildlife: Mostly common deciduous forest birds.

Visitor Activities: Birdwatching; botanizing; viewing prehistoric sites; white-water rafting.

Map labels: Doi Inthanon National Park; To Chiang Mai; Meo Mae Ya Noi; Chom Thong; 108; THAILAND; Bangkok; Nong Ap Chang; Huai Muang; Ob Luang National Park; Mon Hin; Om Khut; 1088; Park Headquarters; Mae Nam Ping; Tha Rua; Ob Luang; 108; N; Hot; To Mae Sariang; Kiu Lom; Wang Lung; 1099; 1103

The Advent of Logging

In the pre-industrial ages, felling of forest was confined to meeting the subsistence needs of small local communities. By the 19th century, however, timber became an internationally traded commodity, which dramatically changed everything. Loggers moved into northern Thailand's forest with elephants and saws, to remove the teak and other commercially valuable timber species (such as *Xylia xylocarpa* and *Pterocarpus macrocarpus*), leaving behind a drier, degraded landscape that has yet to recover. Evidence of this sad period in the history of Thailand's forests can also be seen at Ob Luang. In the early decades of the 20th century, much of Ob Luang National Park was a logging concession granted to the European-based Borneo Company. It felled all the larger trees, particularly teak, and used elephants to drag them to the edge of the gorge. From there, a cable system was used to lower the logs into the river. A dam across the river formed a pool, where the logs were stored until ready to be floated down to the Ping and Chao Phraya rivers, tied together as rafts, eventually for export from Bangkok to Europe. The remains of the cable system and dam can still be seen at the last point on the nature trail.

Recreation and Education

Today, recreation and eco-tourism have superseded logging as the main human use of this forest. Every year thousands of visitors view the exhibition at the park headquarters to learn about northern Thailand's earliest inhabitants. They pick up an informative, colourful

Above: *Large spikes of fruit, which belong to the aroid,* Amorphophallus paeoniifolius, *are a common sight in the ground flora of Ob Luang's deciduous forest.*

Above, right: *The frog* Rana kuhli *prefers streams and ponds at high altitudes.*

which human beings had the tools necessary to start clearing forests on a large scale, paving the way for the arrival of agriculture and a settled existence. With the advent of Iron Age axes, over 2,000 years ago, it became even easier to clear forest and to prevent forest regeneration with fire. A gradual reduction in rainfall also changed the forest from rainforest to the drier forest types seen in the park today. As metal weapons replaced wooden spears, hunters began to have a significant impact on the wildlife.

leaflet (in English or Thai), which guides them around a 1.2-kilometre (¾ mile) circular trail past the archaeological sites and provides a clear introduction to the forest types of the area. The viewpoint, above the rock paintings at the top of Pa Chang, affords a commanding panorama over the remaining deciduous dipterocarp and bamboo deciduous forest. Points along the trail introduce walkers to lichens, termites and various plants, including the wild cliff banana, which grows on the sheer rock faces of the gorge. The final stretch of the nature trail passes along the edge of the gorge, with a sheer drop down to the river 50 metres (164 feet) below. Extreme caution must be exercised there, making the walk unsuitable for young children.

The park headquarters provides a very pleasant area for picnics and for camping. Added attractions include hair-raising raft trips along the Chaem River. Hot springs and another enchanting gorge known as Ob Noi, west of the park headquarters, provide evidence of the geological forces, which continue to uplift the mountains.

Wildlife

A recent survey of mammals in the national park by volunteer Arthur Wright reported 34 species, including both of Thailand's goat species, the Serow and the Goral. The latter is a Himalayan species and is considered highly endangered in Thailand, occurring only west of the Ping River. Three cats are present: Fishing Cat, Leopard Cat and Jungle Cat. Four primates have been recorded: Slow Loris, Rhesus Macaque, Pig-tailed Macaque and White-handed Gibbon. The less-conspicuous smaller mammals include several species of squirrel, mongoose, civet, marten, shrew and the Small-clawed Otter.

Birds are said to number approximately 200 species, but no thorough survey has been completed. They are mostly ubiquitous species of deciduous forests such as barbets, bulbuls, drongos and babblers. Two species that can only be seen along the gorge are the Blue Whistling Thrush and the rare Brown Dipper.

Above, right: *The nocturnal Slow Loris has eyes especially sensitive to dim light, which enables it to find insects, nestling birds and fruit at night.*

Right: *The Tabby is a rare butterfly found from Kashmir to South China and Thailand.*

RAMKHAMHAENG NATIONAL PARK

Spirits Guard the Birthplace of Thai Civilization

Established in 1980, Ramkhamhaeng National Park encompasses an isolated, 341-square-kilometre (131-square-mile) chain of mountains, running south from Sukothai, Thailand's first capital city. At the heart of the park, the summit of Khao Luang rises to 1,200 metres (3,960 feet) above sea level, dominating the surrounding landscape. The main attractions are the hike up Khao Luang, camping near the summit and watching the sun rise over the ruins of ancient Sukothai.

Forests

Wildlife habitats here include mixed evergreen-deciduous forest, bamboo-deciduous forest and

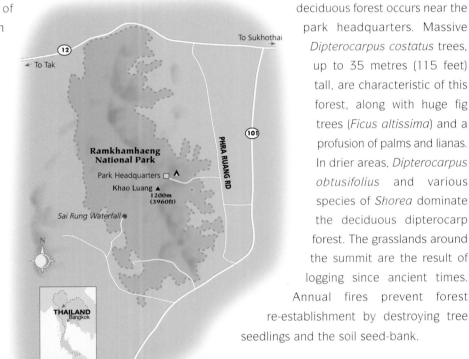

deciduous dipterocarp forest in the lowlands, and degraded grasslands near the summit. A fine example of mixed evergreen deciduous forest occurs near the park headquarters. Massive *Dipterocarpus costatus* trees, up to 35 metres (115 feet) tall, are characteristic of this forest, along with huge fig trees (*Ficus altissima*) and a profusion of palms and lianas. In drier areas, *Dipterocarpus obtusifolius* and various species of *Shorea* dominate the deciduous dipterocarp forest. The grasslands around the summit are the result of logging since ancient times. Annual fires prevent forest re-establishment by destroying tree seedlings and the soil seed-bank.

Wildlife

A total of 86 bird species has been recorded in the park. The best area for birdwatching is the lowland forest, near the park headquarters, where Blue Pitta, Velvet-fronted Nuthatch, Orange-breasted Trogon and Grey-headed Flycatcher are resident. Baya Weaver, Green-billed Malkoha and Stripe-throated Bulbul prefer more open habitats and can be seen along the summit trail. Winter migrants include Forest Wagtail and Common Kingfisher. Centuries of hunting have wiped out most large mammals. Common Wild Pigs are, however, abundant and Barking Deer, Sambar Deer and Asian Wild Dogs are occasionally reported.

Opposite, above: *The original citizens of the ancient city of Sukothai would have relied heavily on the natural resources now protected within Ramkhamhaeng National Park.*

Opposite, below left: *The Green-billed Malkoha is often seen during the ascent of Khao Luang.*

Opposite, below right: *The small Chestnut Rat is a common resident in evergreen forest higher than 900 m elevation.*

Above, right: *Flowers and leaves of* Dipterocarpus obtusifolius *scattered on the deciduous forest floor.*

Location: Southwest of northern Thailand, 20 km (12 miles) south and east of Sukothai.

Climate: Mean annual rainfall 1,360 mm (54 in), falling mostly May–October; mean annual temperature 27°C (81°F); hottest months March–June; coolest November–February. Temperatures on the summit can be uncomfortably cold, especially at night.

When to Go: The cool season (November–February) provides the clearest views and a chance to see winter migrant birds. Avoid public holidays, as the park is a very popular destination for Thai tourists.

Access: Rented or private vehicle. From Sukothai, travel 20 km (12 miles) south on Highway 101 to Kirimat crossroads. Turn right and follow the signs a further 16 km (10 miles) to the park headquarters.

Permits: Entrance fee charged for summit trail. Telephone the park headquarters (055-619200-1) to arrange your visit.

Equipment: For the summit trail, camping equipment and warm clothes; for rambles in the lowlands, light clothes, stout boots and mosquito repellent.

Facilities: At the park headquarters, bungalows, tents for hire, porters available, restaurant, nature trails and a small information centre; campsite near the summit.

Watching Wildlife: Small mammals, squirrels, civets, martens, deer and wild pigs; 86 bird species, mostly common residents of deciduous forest and open areas.

Visitor Activities: Hill walking, camping and birdwatching.

Right: *Nearly every year during the dry season, forest fires sweep through the deciduous forest at the base of Khao Luang burning off the leaf litter and the precious nutrients it contains. Most of the trees, however, survive.*

Reaching the Top

The central feature of the park is the walking trail to the summit. It takes at least four hours to cover the 4 kilometres (2½ miles) from the park headquarters to the campsite near the summit. The path is steep at first and should be attempted only by fit walkers. A viewpoint after 1.2 kilometres (¾ mile) provides vistas for those who do not want to go to the top. Points of interest along the route include large *Pterocarpus macrocarpus* and fig trees, tree ferns and a grove of bamboo. According to local legend, a cave, Plong Nang Nuk, 3.3 kilometres (2 miles) from the trail entrance, links the mountain with the ancient city of Si Satchanalai, some 70 kilometres (43 miles) to the north. It has never been

surveyed. There are four summits, linked by easy foot-paths, each providing a different view over the surrounding countryside. Near the northeastern summit, Pha Na Rai, a massive overhanging boulder provides dramatic photo opportunities.

For the less adventurous, two short circular nature trails (1.2 and 2.0 kilometres – just under and just over 1 mile, respectively), with informative boards, branch off the summit trail near the entrance. A small entrance fee is charged for the summit trail and nature trails.

The Dawn of Thai Civilization

Sukothai Historical Park, a World Heritage Site, lies adjacent to the northeastern boundary of Ramkhamhaeng National Park. Sukothai, capital of the first Thai kingdom, was established in AD1238 and flourished until the late 14th century. The national park is named after the second Sukothai king, Ramkhamhaeng the Great, who reigned over the Golden Age of Siam and is accredited with establishing the Thai form of Buddhism. Khao Luang is still regarded as a sacred mountain by the citizens of modern-day Sukothai. Its spiritual significance probably originates from the dependence of Sukothai's early residents on the mountain's timber and water. Remnants of dams and canals, which irrigated the rice fields surrounding ancient Sukothai, are scattered along the eastern boundary of the park, which is also flanked by Thailand's first trunk road, the Phra Ruang Highway. A powerful guardian spirit is believed to inhabit the mountain. Before ascending Khao Luang, hikers pay homage and pray for their safety at a small shrine near the entrance to the summit trail.

Below: *The swirling roots of a strangling fig tree.*

SRILANNA NATIONAL PARK

A Flooded Forest

Srilanna National Park was created in 1989 to protect the watershed of the Mae Ngud Dam, a project designed to generate electricity, as well as supply irrigation water to rice farmers in the northern province of Chiang Mai. Although the reservoir flooded riverine forest habitat of great value to conservation, the surrounding forest has survived and flourished under the protection of the national park and helped to prevent siltation of the reservoir. The reservoir is, however, only a small part of this 1,406-square-kilometre (543-square-mile) national park, the sixth largest in Thailand. The rest of the park comprises rolling granite hills and outcrops of limestone covered in both deciduous and evergreen forest types, and harbouring waterfalls and caves that are well worth exploring. The park's highest point is Doi Chom Hot, which reaches a maximum elevation of 1,718 metres (5,636 feet). The small town of Phrao and its surrounding rice fields form a large enclave in the middle of the park.

The Reservoir

Mae Ngud Reservoir has a surface area of 20 square kilometres (8 square miles) and is situated in Mae Taeng

Above, right: Red flowers of the naturalized exotic herb Ipomea hederifolia *from tropical America. This plant now readily invades disturbed forest edges all over Asia.*

District of Chiang Mai Province. Recreation facilities on the reservoir are not handled by the park, but are franchised out to private entrepreneurs. From the dam, tourists enjoy scenic rides in traditional long-tailed boats to floating restaurants. When the water is low, the branches of drowned trees emerge above the surface of the water, reminding visitors of the forest diversity that was sacrificed to build the dam. Water birds commonly seen along the way include Lesser Whistling Duck, Great and Intermediate Egrets and Chinese Pond Heron. Fishing and swimming are both allowed in the reservoir. Water, rising behind the dam, engulfed several villages, which were relocated to the north of the reservoir.

Waterfalls

The park contains several beautiful waterfalls on the rivers that drain into the reservoir. They are best observed at the end of the rainy season. Mon Hin Lai Waterfall is probably the most attractive and it is here that water trickles over small steps down a rugged cliff face for a total of 104 metres (341 feet), in a densely forested ravine. Along the path to the falls are magnificent buttressed *Dracontomelon dao* trees, huge fig trees and many wild bananas, which attract civets at night. At the top, there is a viewpoint offering a sweeping panorama over the surrounding countryside, including the enclave of Phrao.

Location: Chiang Mai Province, 50 km (31 miles) north of the provincial capital.

Climate: Monsoonal; rainy season May–October; cool, dry season November–February; hot, dry season March–April (maximum daytime temperatures often exceed 40°C/104°F).

When to Go: The level of the reservoir is highest towards the end of the rainy season. Very high temperatures and smoke from forest fires make the area uncomfortable during the hot, dry season.

Access: By car, follow Highway 107 north from Chiang Mai City 41 km (26 miles) to Mae Taeng. At the large Mae Ngud Reservoir sign, turn east 12 km (7½ miles) to the dam and park headquarters. The park's attractions are scattered over a very large area, many of which can be reached only by four-wheel-drive car.

Permits: An entrance fee is charged near the dam.

Equipment: Sunblock for boating on the reservoir; light clothes and sturdy boots for walking in the forest; swimming gear; waterproofs in the rainy season.

Facilities: Boats, floating accommodation and restaurants are operated on the reservoir; campsites and a raft dormitory; small exhibition at the park headquarters; several nature trails.

Watching Wildlife: A wide variety of forest and waterbirds are the main wildlife attraction; gibbons, barking deer and civets may be seen with luck.

Visitor Activities: Birdwatching; forest walks; boating; visiting waterfalls and caves.

Right: *One of the most popular activities in Srilanna National Park is to take a boat trip on the reservoir to one of many privately operated floating restaurants.*

Below: *Egrets are some of the most typical and easily recognized birds of open countryside in Thailand. Little Egrets are common winter visitors to the paddy fields and reservoirs of the north.*

Pa Daeng

A valley hemmed in by dramatic limestone cliffs, with several hill-tribe communities and an attractive cave, provides scenic and cultural highlights in the northwest of the park, accessible via a dirt track running east from Highway 107 near the small town of Chiang Dhao. The main ethnic groups of this area are the Karen and the Lahu. The Karen still rely heavily on intact forest to supply many of their basic needs, but the Lahu have cleared forest at the edge of the park for cultivation of corn. A project by Wildlife Fund Thailand is attempting to help the villagers to develop more sustainable agricultural practices and to encourage them to become involved in tree-planting programmes to restore the buffer zone. The Lions Club has also sponsored tree planting in the national park, as part of celebrations to mark the King's Golden Jubilee.

Wildlife

The park's fauna remains largely undocumented, but it is unlikely to include many large species. According to park rangers, a few White-handed Gibbons and Sambar Deer still survive in the more remote areas. Various squirrels, civets, porcupines, Common Barking Deer, Common Wild Pig and Burmese Ferret-badger undoubtedly occur. Birds are mostly those common in deciduous forest, including several species of bulbul, barbet, drongo, babbler, warbler and flycatcher.

Above: *Wild bananas are giant herbs and an abundant, year-round food source in northern Thailand's forest. They are relied upon by squirrels and civets when other foods are seasonally scarce.*

Left: *Lesser Whistling Ducks often form large flocks on northern Thailand's lakes and ponds, especially in the cool season. The species is named after its repetitive whistling call, uttered in flight.*

THUNG SALAENG LUANG NATIONAL PARK

Flower Meadows and a Refuge for Rebels

Established in 1963 as Thailand's third national park, Thung Salaeng Luang protects 1,262 square kilometres (487 square miles) of forested mountains, reaching a maximum elevation of 1,028 metres (3,372 feet), as well as attractive flower meadows, in Thailand's lower northern region.

Kaeng Sopa Waterfalls

The scenic highlight of the park is Kaeng Sopa Waterfalls, near Km 71 on Highway 12. In a country where the attractiveness of waterfalls tends

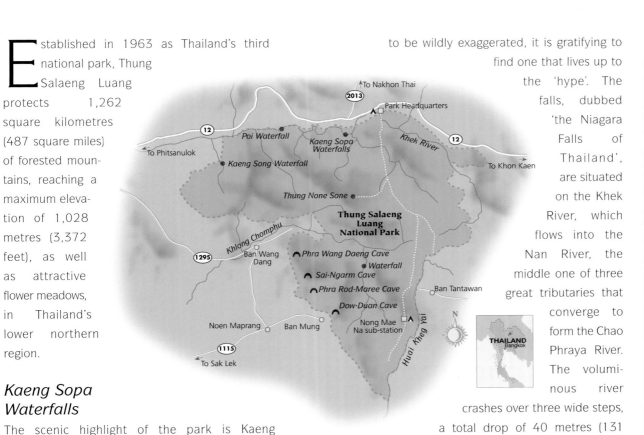

to be wildly exaggerated, it is gratifying to find one that lives up to the 'hype'. The falls, dubbed 'the Niagara Falls of Thailand', are situated on the Khek River, which flows into the Nan River, the middle one of three great tributaries that converge to form the Chao Phraya River. The voluminous river crashes over three wide steps, a total drop of 40 metres (131 feet), with spray and thunder, even in the dry season.

The Meadows

Although most of the park is covered by deciduous dipterocarp and mixed evergreen-deciduous forest, it is the open pine savannahs (*thung* in Thai), occupying a mere two per cent of the park's area, that are the central feature. They support varied communities of wildflowers and provide grazing for wildlife. Frequent fires, shallow soils and seasonal drought maintain these grasslands. Thung Salaeng Luang, which lends its name to the national park, is itself named after a small, fire-resistant tree species, *Strychnos nux-vomica*, which is common on the grassland. The seeds of this tree contain strychnine,

Opposite, above: *Open grasslands* (thung *in Thai) studded with pine trees are the main features at Thung Salaeng Luang.*

Opposite, below left: Mussaenda parva, *a common and widespread shrub in both deciduous and evergreen forest types, flowers in the cool, dry season.*

Opposite, below right: *Thung Salaeng Luang is famous for its butterflies. This species is* Euthalia pardalis.

Above, right: *The Silver-breasted Broadbill constructs a delicately woven nest, hanging from the flimsiest tree branches, often over water, to avoid predators.*

Location: In the provinces of Phitsanulok and Phetchabun, about 60 km (37 miles) east of Phitsanulok.

Climate: Monsoonal; mean annual rainfall 1,200-2,000 mm (47-78 in); mean annual temperature approximately 27°C (81°F); rainy season May–October; cool, dry season November–January; hot, dry season February–April (mean monthly temperature over 30°C/86°F).

When to Go: October to February, best for wild flowers, waterfalls and large mammals.

Access: The park headquarters is reached by travelling 79 km (49 miles) east along Highway 12, from the provincial capital, Phitsanulok. Public buses between Phitsanulok and Khon Kaen stop near Kaeng Sopa Falls and the park headquarters.

Permits: None required. Entrance fees at waterfalls.

Equipment: Insect repellent; strong shoes and light clothes for forest walks; a torch for caves; waterproof gear.

Facilities: Bungalows for six to 14 people for rent at park headquarters and Nong Mae Na substation; several campsites; visitor centre with small exhibition at park headquarters; resorts and restaurants along Highway 12; nature trails and long-distance treks with guides. Visitors should keep to marked paths, because of landmines.

Watching Wildlife: Excellent birdwatching, butterfly spotting and botanizing.

Visitor Activities: Forest walks; visiting waterfalls and caves; birdwatching.

Right: Livistona *palms can still sometimes be seen in evergreen forest along streams and rivers, but they are under considerable pressure from the horticultural trade.*

Below: *Rather extravagantly dubbed the 'Niagara Falls' of Thailand, the magnificent Kaeng Sopa Waterfalls are one of the scenic highlights of the national park.*

one of the world's most powerful nerve toxins. Another botanical feature of this area is the parasitic plant *Christisonia siamensis*, a species endemic to Thailand, which feeds on grass roots. Its white tubular flowers, rimmed with dark purple-and-yellow spots, appear to sit directly on the soil surface.

A trek of 20 kilometres (12.5 miles) through evergreen forest leads to Thung None Sone, at the heart of the national park, a beautiful savannah studded with pine trees and *Phoenix* palms. These palms rise from the ashes of the fires that sweep across the savannah every dry season. Their growing points are insulated against the flames by being sunken within the woody stem of the plant and surrounded by dead leaf stalks. After fire, new green leaves sprout from the blackened plant. Colourful herbs, such as the purple *Barleria strigosa* and *Pseuderanthemum andersonii*, insect-eating pitcher plants, ground orchids and gingers also provide interest for botanists.

Small mammals include Yellow-throated Marten, Masked Palm Civet, Black Giant Squirrel, Long-tailed Macaque and Dusky Langur. White-handed Gibbons can still be found in more remote areas of the park, but their population has recently crashed to just a handful of individuals.

A total of 203 bird species have been confirmed within the national park, including several rare birds of prey such as Mountain Hawk Eagle, White-rumped Falcon and Peregrine Falcon. Other interesting bird species include Great Hornbill, Great Slaty Woodpecker, Coral-billed Ground Cuckoo and Silver-breasted Broadbill.

The Sad Story of Schombugk's Deer

Thung Salaeng Luang may have been the last stronghold of Schombugk's Deer, a species endemic to Thailand. It became extinct in the 1930s, the only deer species to have disappeared since the Stone Age. With large, splayed hooves and spreading antlers, this deer species lived on open swampy plains and grasslands, avoiding

Left: Some of the meadows in Thung Salaeng Luang National Park are studded with Phoenix loureiri Palms, named after their ability to regrow rapidly after fire. The fruits are edible.

Below: The open meadows of Thung Salaeng Luang National Park provide almost perfect conditions for spotting large mammals, such as wild cattle, deer and occasionally elephants.

Fauna

The open grasslands and savannahs of Thung Salaeng Luang provide excellent grazing for the park's large herbivores, and good opportunities for wildlife enthusiasts to view these animals in fairly open conditions. At dusk, Common Barking Deer, Sambar Deer and the occasional Gaur emerge from the surrounding forest to graze on the meadows, whilst Common Wild Pigs root around for corms and tubers. Siamese Hares are abundant and can often be seen in the daytime. Such animals provide prey for Asian Wild Dogs and perhaps the occasional Tiger. Although no one has seen a Tiger for quite some time, Tiger tracks are still reported by park rangers. A small herd of Asian Elephants is resident within the park and has increased its numbers from about 20 in the 1980s to about 30 today. The park authority is establishing new salt licks to encourage Asian Elephants and other large mammals not to migrate outside the park and cause conflict with surrounding farmers.

dense forests, which restricted its movement. It was fairly common in open areas at Thung Salaeng Luang until the 1920s. The last reported wild Schombugk's Deer was shot in 1932 in Kanchanaburi Province. Monks at a temple in Samut Sakorn cared for a free-ranging tame male, possibly the last of its kind, as late as 1938, but a drunkard, who mistook it for a wild deer, clubbed it to death.

Other Attractions

Along the western boundary of the park are four limestone caves, which make interesting destinations for long-distance hikers. Butterflies are also an attraction. The area around Wang Nam Yen rapids is said to be especially rewarding for butterfly watchers. Thung Salaeng Luang was a stronghold of Communist insurgents from the late 1960s to the early 1980s. The deciding battles between Communist and Government forces took place at Khao Khor to the east of the park, where the Communists were finally defeated in 1982. Part of a Communist settlement and rice fields have, however, been preserved in the southeast of the park and are now features on an excellent nature trail, which starts at the Nong Mae Na substation. Landmines from this period are still occasionally unearthed in the park, so walkers should not stray from the paths.

Above: Ardesia crenata, *an evergreen treelet, produces edible fruits relished by birds and mammals from August to February.*

Right: *Streams like this become an important refuge for wildlife during the dry season. Forests by streams usually support more species than dry forests and are very important for the conservation of biodiversity.*

Opposite: *The Black Giant Squirrel feeds on fruits and seeds in the treetops, rarely venturing to the ground. It is capable of leaping long distances between trees.*

NORTHEASTERN THAILAND (ISAAN)

At first glance, northeastern Thailand, or Isaan as it is known locally, seems an unpromising destination for nature lovers. Agriculture is the main activity, but a dry climate and poor soils make life difficult for farmers. Isaan is the most impoverished region in the country, forcing local people to overexploit natural resources. The region has the lowest forest cover in the country (12 per cent) and wildlife has a hard time surviving habitat loss and hunting.

The Khorat Plateau, a gently undulating, mostly sandstone landscape, forms most of Isaan. Rivers drain eastwards into the Mekong River, which marks the northern and eastern boundary of the region. Mountain ranges form the western and southern boundaries, and contain the best protected areas.

Khao Yai, at the western end of the Phanom Dongrak mountain range, is not only the nation's oldest park, but it is also one of the most accessible. Its abundant, visible wildlife attracts huge numbers of visitors. East from Khao Yai, Thap Lan National Park is more degraded, but this quieter park retains healthy populations of large mammals, and is the location of impressive attempts to restore forest ecosystems.

The western part of the region is dominated by majestic, flat-topped, sandstone mountains, or mesas, two of which – Phu Kradung and Phu Rua – are described here. Their main attractions are a profusion of unusual plants.

And then there are the dinosaurs. Isaan is becoming a top attraction for palaeontologists, as new dinosaur fossils are unearthed, and Phu Wiang National Park provides an opportunity to take an imaginary journey back to the Age of the Dinosaurs.

KHAO YAI NATIONAL PARK

Thailand's Premier Tropical Forest Park

Created in September 1962, Thailand's first national park, Khao Yai, protects a large remnant (2,168 square kilometres/836 square miles) of a vast forest, which once covered most of northeastern Thailand. Most of the forest was cleared to make way for rapid agricultural development after the Second World War and for road building during the Vietnamese War, but thanks to the tireless campaigning of Thailand's foremost naturalist, the late Dr Boonsong Lekagul, Khao Yai was saved from destruction. It now appears on satellite images as an isolated island of forest in a sea of agricultural land.

Khao Yai retains excellent forest and wildlife and

Opposite, above: *This campsite affords a rare sideways view of the forest structure at Khao Yai.*

Opposite, below left: *Silver Pheasants can be seen in evergreen forest around the park headquarters.*

Opposite, below right: *The Pileated Gibbon is one of Thailand's many endangered species.*

Above, right: Urena lobata *is a common weedy herb found throughout Isaan in disturbed areas.*

Previous pages:
Page 110: *An open grassland in Phu Kiew Wildlife Sanctuary.* Page 111: *Gibbon calls are perhaps the most evocative sound of Thailand's forests.*

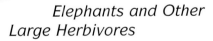

provides the most accessible location for eco-tourists to view large mammals in Thailand. It plays host to 71 mammal species (including at least 16 bats), more than one-third of Thailand's bird species (at least 340), at least 189 butterflies and an estimated 2,500 vascular plant species.

A large part of the park is a rolling plateau of sandstone, ranging in elevation from 600 to 1,000 metres (1,968–3,281 feet). Some of the river valleys, however, lie as low as 60 metres (197 feet) above sea level, and the highest peak, Khao Rom, is 1,351 metres (4,433 feet) above sea level.

Elephants and Other Large Herbivores

The park is mostly covered by dense, primary, evergreen forest, with small areas of open grassland, the result of cultivation by villagers and bandits, long since evicted from the park, and an abandoned golf course. Although 'unnatural', these areas provide essential grazing for the park's large herbivores and give visitors excellent opportunities to view wildlife. Deer can sometimes be seen grazing in the open in broad daylight, but it is during the evening that these grasslands come alive with Asian Elephants, Sambar Deer, Common Barking Deer, Common Wild Pigs and Gaurs. Wildlife is easily seen from the road or from wildlife observation towers.

Khao Yai is undoubtedly the best site in Thailand to see Asian Elephants in their natural habitat. It is estimated that 140–200 elephants live in the park. Their footprints and dung can be seen everywhere. Elephants

Location: 200 km (125 miles) northeast of Bangkok, in Saraburi, Prachinburi, Nakhon Ratchasima and Nakhon Nayok provinces.

Climate: Monsoonal; mean annual temperature 23°C (73°F); mean annual rainfall 1,600-3,000 mm (63-118 in); rainy season May–October; cool season November–January (average temperature 17°C/63°F); hot, dry season February–April (average temperature 28°C/82°F).

When to Go: Any time of the year.

Access: By car northeast from Bangkok on Highway 1, then Highway 2 to Pak Chong, turning south on Highway 2090, 25 km (15½ miles) to the park headquarters. Public buses to Nakhon Ratchasima run every 30–60 minutes from Bangkok's Morchit Bus Station, stopping at Pak Chong, from where pickup-truck taxis run to the park entrance.

Permits: An entrance fee is charged.

Equipment: Protection against leeches and mosquitoes; camping equipment; light clothes and tough shoes for forest walks, and warm clothes in the cool season; waterproofs.

Facilities: Most visitors stay in resorts and campsites outside the park, near the northern entrance. Park bungalows are available only for researchers and officials; campsites and tents for rent; four small restaurants; visitor centre with exhibition; many marked trails.

Watching Wildlife: Asian Elephants, deer, wild cattle, primates and hornbills.

Visitor Activities: Forest walks, watching wildlife, botanizing, rafting and cycling.

Above: *The White-handed Gibbon exists in two colour variations; a light form and a dark one, shown here. Pairings usually occur between individuals of the same colour form. Genes for the dark fur are dominant over those for light fur.*

Above, right: *The light colour form of the White-handed Gibbon. It's disproportionately long arms and strong grasping hands enable it to swing with ease from branch to branch, a form of locomotion known as brachiation.*

are particularly common along the road, which bisects the park, between Km 25 and Km 35. Several salt licks in this area attract not only elephants but also many other animals, best observed at dawn or dusk. To view nocturnal wildlife, the park headquarters organizes 'spotlight safaris'. Visitors are driven around the park at night in trucks mounted with powerful lamps and are almost guaranteed sightings of deer, Asian Elephants, giant flying squirrels, civets, porcupines, bats and many other species.

Reports of up to 50 Tigers living in the park continue to circulate, but recent surveys indicate that very few Tigers survive there. Other cats present include Leopard, Leopard Cat, Clouded Leopard and the highly endangered Marbled Cat, but sightings of all these species are exceedingly rare.

Gibbons

Khao Yai is the only place where two of Thailand's gibbon species, the White-handed and the Pileated, come into contact. The White-handed Gibbon is distributed from Sumatra through Malaysia to northern Thailand, Yunnan and parts of Laos. This species has two colour forms,

either light tan, or dark brown to black, and is distinguished by a white ring completely surrounding the facial features. Pileated Gibbons, restricted to eastern Thailand, Laos and Cambodia, are sexually dimorphic. Mature males are black, whilst mature females are buff with a black crown, throat and chest. The two species have different songs. White-handed Gibbons rouse campers with soaring, melodious whoops, whereas the song of the Pileated Gibbon is similar to the beat of a drum. Although rare, interbreeding between the species does sometimes occur, with the hybrid offspring singing an intermediate song. Khao Yai is home to the longest continuous study of gibbons in the world. Teams from Mahidol University (led by Dr Warren Brockelman) and from the Max Plank Institute for Biological Anthropology (led by Dr Ulrich Reichard) have been observing gibbon family life and studying their habitat needs there for more than 20 years.

Other primates in the park include the Slow Loris and Pig-tailed Macaques; the latter roam around the park in large troops. Asian Wild Dogs can occasionally be seen hunting deer in packs. Both the Asiatic Black Bear and Malayan Sunbear also occur.

Left: Massive emergent trees soar above the main canopy of the evergreen forest that is characteristic of Khao Yai.

Below, left: A signboard in the Khao Yai National Park alerts visitors to the presence of Tigers.

Below: Although Thailand's Tiger population has been much reduced in recent years, a few still remain in Khao Yai, particularly around the park headquarters.

Hornbills

Khao Yai is an important research site for hornbills. Dr Pilai Poonswad and her team from Mahidol University have been conducting long-term studies on the diet and breeding ecology of hornbills in Khao Yai since the early 1980s. Four species live in the park: Wreathed, Brown, Oriental Pied and Great. Hornbills are primarily frugivorous, with figs comprising a large part of their diet, but they can also take insects and small reptiles, especially during the breeding season. They survive only in undisturbed forest with large trees, since they nest in large holes in tree trunks. The females seal themselves inside the nesting cavity, blocking the entrance with faeces and other materials, leaving only a narrow slit, through which the male passes food. Females begin their imprisonment in January to March and the chicks usually fledge in May or June. Outside the breeding season, Wreathed Hornbills provide Khao Yai's most impressive bird spectacle, as they start to congregate together in flocks, small at first but gradually increasing to contain up to 1,000 individuals. They come together to feed and roost in the largest forest trees.

Below: *The Great Hornbill is Thailand's largest hornbill species. Its huge bill and wide gape enable it to disperse the largest of tree seeds.*

In addition to hornbills, the park boasts an impressive array of rare birds of prey, including Peregrine Falcon, Mountain Hawk Eagle, Rufous-bellied Eagle, Grey-headed Fish-eagle and Buffy Fish-owl. Among the park's other notable birds are Narcissus Flycatcher, Silver Oriole, Coral-billed Ground Cuckoo, Oriental Cuckoo, Yellow-footed Pigeon, Silver Pheasant, Siamese Fireback, Blue and Eared Pittas, Orange-breasted and Red-headed Trogons and four species of broadbill.

Activities and Attractions

Wildlife watching is by far the most popular activity in Khao Yai, usually undertaken by hiking along the myriad of well-marked trails which radiate out from the park headquarters, ranging in length from 1.5–8 kilometres (1–5 miles). In addition, several waterfalls are well worth a visit, the tallest and most spectacular of which is Haew Narok, which plummets 80 metres (262 feet) in two huge leaps. Haew Suwat is another popular waterfall on the upper reaches of the Lam Takhong River. The rivers provide opportunities for white-water rafting along the park's southeastern boundary. Exhilarating trips of up to three hours can be arranged. Mountain biking is also being promoted in the park; bicycles can be rented from the national park headquarters. Advised routes take cyclists past most of the wildlife viewing points around the centre of the park.

Above: *Large troops of Pig-tailed Macaques, with up to 40 individuals, roam widely throughout the park.*

Below, left: *The Siamese Fireback can be seen in evergreen forest around the national park headquarters.*

Below: *The white ear patch shows that this Red Jungle-fowl belongs to the eastern subspecies. It is a close relative of the domestic chicken.*

PHU KRADUNG NATIONAL PARK

Mountains, Pine Forests and Flower Meadows

A tough mountain trek, with the reward of sweeping panoramas and romantic pine forests and flower meadows, is the main attraction of Phu Kradung National Park. Spread over 348 square kilometres (134 square miles) of Loei Province, Phu Kradung is Thailand's second national park, declared just two months after Khao Yai, in November 1962. This massive, flat-topped, sandstone mountain, 1,325 metres (4,347 feet) high, is capped with a 60-square-kilometre (23-square-mile) plateau. The mountain probably received its name from its bell-like shape (*kradung* means bell in Thai), but an alternative derivation is provided by folklore that tells of bells rung by spirits that echo from the mountain on certain Buddhist holy days. The park is a haven for plant species that prefer a cooler climate.

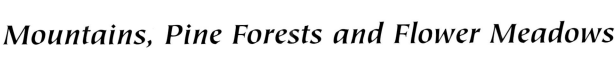

Opposite, above: *Phu Kradung from a distance, showing the typical flat-topped structure of the sandstone hills or 'mesas' of north-east Thailand.*

Opposite, below left: *The Blue Pansy is a very attractive, common and widespread butterfly.*

Opposite, below right: *Students stride through the pine savanna that typifies Phu Kradung's plateau.*

Above, right: *The ground orchid* Arundina graminifolia *is characteristic of degraded deciduous forest.*

A Test of Love

It is said that lovers who help each other to reach the top of Phu Kradung will stay together forever, but if they quarrel along the way, they are destined to separate. The trek up the mountain begins at the lower park office, where porters congregate to carry the belongings of trekkers in bundles on the end of bamboo poles. After hiring porters, intrepid mountaineers pay a fee at the entrance to the summit trail and begin their ascent. The climb is very steep in many places. The footsteps of the many thousands who have made this climb have eroded the path into a muddy gully up to 15 metres (50 feet) wide in places. Aware of the erosion problem, the park authority plans to build concrete steps along steeper sections of the route. Proposals to build a cable car up the mountain come and go. It is a 9-kilometre (6-mile) climb to the edge of the plateau and a further 4 kilometres (2½ miles) from there to the upper park headquarters and campsite. Villagers sell refreshments along the route, which takes three to six hours to complete. The reward is more than 50 kilometres (31 miles) of marked trails, which meander around the plateau, leading to cliffs with stunning views, impressive waterfalls and beautiful meadows of wildflowers.

Plateau Vegetation

The most interesting plant communities in the park occur on the plateau, which is covered with rolling savannah,

Location: Loei Province, 70 km (44 miles) south of the provincial capital.

Climate: Monsoonal; mean annual temperature 26°C (79°F); mean annual rainfall 1,215 mm (48 in); rainy season May–September (19–21 rainy days per month); cool season October–January (minimum temperature 13°C/55°F, but falling to freezing on the plateau); hot, dry season February–April (maximum temperature 36°C/97°F).

When to Go: The park is closed from June to September. October to January is the most popular time to visit the park, but it becomes very overcrowded.

Access: By car, from Loei, travel 82 km (51 miles) south on Highway 201, turning west at Km 276 on Highway 2019, 8 km (4 miles) to the lower park office. Phu Kradung plateau can be accessed only on foot. Buses from Bangkok's Eastern Bus Terminal stop at Amphoe Phu Kradung, from where local buses can be hired to the park headquarters.

Permits: An entrance fee is charged.

Equipment: Warm clothes are essential, especially during the cool season; camping equipment.

Facilities: On the plateau, tents and bungalows for rent, restaurant and store; porters; signposted nature trails; visitor centre with exhibition.

Watching Wildlife: Orchids, rhododendrons and carnivorous plants; Asian Elephants, deer, gibbons and squirrels; more than 150 bird species.

Visitor Activities: Botanizing, birdwatching and hiking.

maintained by fire, and studded with pine trees. Both of Thailand's two native pine species grow there. Most common is the two-needled pine (*Pinus merkusii*), whilst the three-needled pine (*P. kesiya*) is much rarer. The ground is carpeted with wildflowers, providing an ever-changing show of colour. Particularly attractive are the dense clusters of pinkish-white *Curcuma angustifolia* (a member of the ginger family), which blooms prolifically in burnt areas during April. The ground flora includes several species of genera more usually associated with temperate climates, such as gentians and violets. Phu Kradung is also famous for both ground orchids, which tend to flower in the rainy season, and epiphytic orchids (growing on trees), which mostly flower during the late dry season. Several species of *Dendrobium*, *Cymbidium*, *Eria*, *Habenaria* and fabulous lady's slipper orchids add variety to the botanical spectacle.

Insect-eating Plants

Curious carnivorous plants are one of the most interesting features of the ground flora. The soil on the plateau of Phu Kradung is poor in nutrients. Carnivorous plants overcome this problem by digesting insects and absorbing nutrients from their bodies. Three species of pitcher plant grow amongst the grass. They develop modified pitcher-like leaves, filled with a digestive 'soup'. Insects, attracted by the sweet fragrance of nectar, lose their footing on the smooth, waxy walls of the pitchers, falling into the fluid that they contain. The bodies of the drowned insects are rapidly digested and the plant absorbs the nutrients thus released. Sundews, of which there are two species in the park, trap insects on leaves covered with hairs that are tipped with beads of sticky fluid. The fluid not only acts as glue, but also contains enzymes which digest the trapped insects. The hairs then absorb the released nutrients.

Relic Evergreen Forest

Small patches of the original evergreen forest that once covered the entire plateau still survive. These relic forests abound with tree species more reminiscent of temperate latitudes, such as oaks, chestnuts, birches and hornbeams. They also support curious Gymnosperm tree species (*Podocarpus neriifolius* and *Cephalotaxus griffithii*), living fossils from the age of the dinosaurs, that are now exceedingly rare in Thailand. Several species of maple carpet trails with crimson fallen leaves in December. Both white and red rhododendrons (*Rhododendron lyi* and *R. simsii*) are common, producing attractive blooms from January to April

Above: *Many of the villagers who live near Phu Kradung make a living as porters, carrying the belongings of tourists, perfectly balanced on the ends of bamboo poles, up the mountain.*

Right: *A serene sunset viewed through pine trees from the plateau of Phu Kradung. The peaceful atmosphere of the plateau makes the climb worthwhile.*

Left: *Lady's slipper orchids, such as this* Paphiopedilum villosum *growing on a* Lithocarpus elegans *tree are amongst the most beautiful flowers of the forest. They are also endangered due to over-collection for the horticulture trade.*

Below: *The brilliant crimson leaves of Maple* (Acer calcaratum) *add a splash of colour to the forest floor when they fall in the dry season.*

Animals

Although plants are the main attraction of Phu Kradung, the park retains small populations of large mammals. A few Asian Elephants still inhabit the quieter northwestern slopes of the park. Common Wild Pig, Common Barking Deer, White-handed Gibbon and Long-tailed Macaque are still fairly common, and Sambar Deer, Serow and even Tiger, although rarely seen, may still inhabit the park. In the canopy of remnant forest patches, Common Tree Shrew and Black Giant Squirrels can be seen.

Birds are much more evident. A total of 152 species of resident and migrant birds have been recorded within the park. Notable rarities include Rufous-bellied Eagle and Nepal House-martin. Among the many winter migrants are Orange-flanked Bush-robin, Mugimaki Flycatcher and Slaty-backed Flycatcher.

PHU WIANG NATIONAL PARK

Thailand's Dinosaur Park

Throughout geological history, central and north-eastern Thailand have alternated between dry land and shallow sea. Around 130 to 140 million years ago, during the early Cretaceous Period, the area that is now Phu Wiang National Park was probably a shallow, brackish-water lagoon, with abundant shellfish, surrounded by mud flats. On higher, dry land nearby, forests of soaring gymnosperm trees grew with an understorey of cycads and fern trees, providing food for enormous browsing sauropod dinosaurs, up to 20 metres (66 feet) in length. In the undergrowth, small ostrich-like theropod dinosaurs (*Compsognathus* in the family Ornithomimidae), each weighing about 3 kilograms (6½ pounds), pursued their prey in packs, whilst trying to avoid becoming meals for predatory tyrannosaurs (*Siamotyrannus isanensis*). Near the water's edge, larger theropods (*Siamosauros suteethorni*) went fishing, some falling prey to huge crocodiles that lurked in the lagoon. Other dinosaurs walked along the shores of the lagoon, leaving their footprints in the baking mud, to be found 140 million years later by palaeontologists.

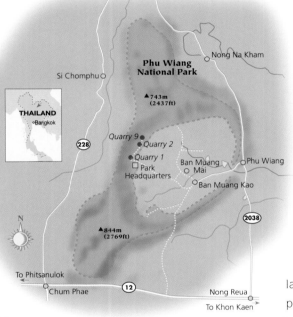

Opposite, above: The glorious yellow flowers of Cassia fistula *are a common sight in Thailand's deciduous forests from March until May. This tree species is commonly planted as a roadside ornamental due to its resistance to pollution.*

Opposite, below left: Although few Dinosaur fossils are on display, an exhibition at Phu Wiang's visitor centre aids the imagination.

Opposite, below right: The Eurasian Jay is a resident in northern and eastern Thailand.

Above, right: The Rufescent Prinia searches for insects amongst the undergrowth of disturbed forest or open areas.

Digging up Geological History

We know all this thanks to the patient excavations by the members of a dedicated team of Thai and French palaeontologists who, since 1982, have brought this ancient world to life. Small pieces of dinosaur bones were first discovered at Phu Wiang in 1982. In 1987, further excavations unearthed almost the whole skeleton of a massive sauropod dinosaur, later confirmed as a new species, named *Phuwiangosaurus sirindhonae*. Another important discovery followed in 1993, when palaeontologists discovered the left hip and 13 vertebrae of a large carnivorous dinosaur, which was estimated to be about 125 million years

Location: Khon Kaen Province, about 55 km (34 miles) west of the provincial capital.

Climate: Monsoonal; rainy season May–October; cool season November–January; hot, dry season February–April.

When to Go: The cool season is the most comfortable time of year for forest walks.

Access: By car, travel west from Khon Kaen, 49 km (31 miles) along Highway 12, to Nong Reua, then north along Highway 2038 to Phu Wiang District Town and then west at Wat Na Yom Wararam, 9 km (6 miles) to the park headquarters. No public transport.

Permits: An entrance fee is charged.

Equipment: Light clothes and tough shoes for trekking to excavation sites; protection against malaria.

Facilities: There is no accommodation or catering for tourists at the park; camping is allowed at the headquarters with permission, but campers must bring all their supplies; dinosaur exhibition; nature trails.

Watching Wildlife: Deer, civets, 147 bird species.

Visitor Activities: Visiting fossil excavation sites; forest walks; birdwatching.

old, and was also subsequently accepted as a species new to science. *Siamotyrannus isanensis* is the oldest tyrannosaur ever found and indicates that this group of ferocious predators probably originated in Asia. Much later, 68 to 65 million years ago, tyrannosaurs became widespread in North America, represented by the much more famous species *Tyrannosaurus rex*. At about 6.5 m (21 feet) in length and weighing a massive two tons, *S. isanensis* was about half the length and one-third the weight of its more imposing North American cousin.

News of the discovery of dinosaurs attracted a flood of visitors, up to 1,000 a day on public holidays, to this formerly little-known national park. The hip of the tyrannosaur was removed to France, and excavation sites are now protected under concrete shelters. Thieves, however, have plundered Phu Wiang, and many of Thailand's other fossil sites, not only to sell the valuable fossils, but also to make charms from the petrified bones. Some people believe that wearing a Buddha image carved from fossilized bone will make them invulnerable to knives and bullets.

Visiting the Excavations

Phu Wiang National Park was established in 1991 to protect not only the fossil sites, but also the surrounding 325 square kilometres (125 square miles) of low mountains covered in deciduous forest. Visitors usually begin their trip to Phu Wiang by perusing the informative exhibition at the park headquarters, which displays a small collection of fossils and models of the dinosaurs. Well-marked trails lead visitors from the headquarters to the excavation sites, where reproductions of the fossils can be seen. A 2.5-kilometre (one-and-a-half-mile) self-guided nature trail leads from the headquarters to Quarries 1 and 2, where sauropod skeletons and teeth of the fish-eating therapod have been unearthed. Above

Left: *The Black-crested Bulbul is a common resident throughout Thailand, living in all forest types from the lowlands to the higlands. Nesting in the undergrowth, it is vulnerable to predators.*

the extraordinarily elaborate concrete structure that now protects one of the excavation sites are rock beds encrusted with fossil shellfish and a small sandstone cave, from which bats emerge at dusk. Quarry 9, where the tyrannosaur was found, is a short but steep scramble through the forest from Quarry 1.

Phu Wiang is an extraordinary landform. It looks like a massive crater or basin encircled by two, almost perfectly concentric, rings of hills or low mountains. The inner circle is highly fragmented and rises to only 470 metres (1,547 feet) above sea level. The outer ring is almost complete, rising to 844 metres (2,769 feet) above sea level, except for a narrow break, providing the only road access point into the inner basin. The floor of the basin is rich agricultural land and is excluded from the national park.

Vegetation and Fauna

More than half of the park is covered by deciduous dipterocarp forest. Bamboo deciduous forest and mixed evergreen deciduous forest, however, and smaller areas of evergreen forest near streams, add to the park's habitat diversity.

The fauna of the area has not been comprehensively surveyed, but at least 147 bird species have been recorded, mostly common residents, such as Black-crested Bulbul, Common Flameback, Shikra, Lineated Barbet, Eurasian Jay, Rufescent Prinia and Green-billed Malkoha, but also including a few rarities (e.g. Siamese Fireback). The park lacks large mammals, but retains smaller species, including Common Barking Deer, Common Wild Pig, Slow Loris, Large and Small Indian Civets, Common and Masked Palm Civets, Lesser Mouse Deer, Fishing Cat, and Crestless Himalayan Porcupine.

Below: *The Masked Palm Civet feeds at night, roaming the forest canopy for fruit, leaves and small animals.*

Phu Rua National Park

Pines, Orchids and Rhododendrons

With its strange rock formations, natural rock gardens smothered in orchids and rhododendrons, and sweeping vistas over a sandstone landscape, Phu Rua provides a quiet retreat for botanists and birdwatchers seeking to avoid the crowds found in the more popular national parks of northeastern Thailand. This small national park (121 square kilometres/ 47 square miles), declared in 1979, protects one of several flat-topped, sandstone mountains (termed mesas by geologists) that dominate the western part of northeastern Thailand. The park is named after a cliff, shaped like the bow of a Chinese junk, which juts out from the mountain (*rua* means boat in Thai).

The plateau, rising to a maximum elevation of 1,365 metres (4,478 feet), with pine trees, open savannah-like

Opposite, above: *Stunted, degraded deciduous forest now covers most of Phu Rua.*

Opposite, below left: *The Brown-throated Sunbird feeds on nectar from flowers.*

Opposite, below right: Etlingera littoralis *is one of the most common large gingers found along streams in Thailand.*

Above, right: Rhododendron simsii *is a speciality of the mountains of Thailand's northeast.*

areas and an abundance of orchids, supports many of the plant species found on the more famous nearby mountain of Phu Kradung. Unlike the latter, however, the summit of Phu Rua can be reached by car. The park, therefore, provides a more accessible alternative to botanists who do not wish to undertake the arduous walk up Phu Kradung, with its throngs of tourists.

Natural Rockeries

The vegetation of Phu Rua has been highly degraded by regular fires and chopping of trees, but this disturbance has created an open pine forest and savannah with a highly diverse ground flora. Particularly interesting are the communities of plants growing on rocks. Periodically, cliff faces crumble, spilling boulders over large areas and creating natural rockeries. At first such boulders become covered in bright orange lichens that, when they decompose, start to provide a thin soil, in which other, larger plants can become rooted.

The plant communities that develop on such rocks are termed epilithic by botanists. At Phu Rua, rhododendrons (*Rhododendron lyi*) are the most dominant epilithic plants. They often smother the boulders, creating a brilliant display of snowy white flowers, tinged with pink, in March and April. Red rhododendrons (*R. simsii*)

LAOS

THAILAND

THAILAND
•Bangkok

Phu Rua National Park

Phu Rua ▲
1365m
(4478ft)

Park Headquarters ▢

Phu Rua ○

 203

To Loei

Ban Gok Nam ○

N

Above: Rhododendrons, orchids, gingers and a wide range of other flowering plants contribute to the high botanical diversity of Phu Rua's natural rock gardens. Rhododendron lyi, pictured here, reaches maximum magnificence in March and April.

also grow in the park, flowering in January and February. It is, however, the profusion of orchids, flowering mainly during the dry season, which are the main attractions of the rock gardens. *Eria albidotomentosa* and *Doritis pulcherima* are among the commoner species, the latter producing delicate spikes of pink flowers on mossy rocks. Several orchid species can be found growing on tree branches (epiphytes) as well as on rocks, including several species of *Dendrobium* and *Bulbophyllum*. In open, mossy patches the carnivorous sundew *Drosera peltata* grows, its sticky leaves trapping unwary insects. In amongst the boulders, ground squirrels scurry, looking for food that is inaccessible to most other animals.

Legendary Rock Formations

Wind and rain easily erode sandstone. This has led to the formation of several strangely shaped monoliths scattered throughout the park. According to local folklore the most famous formation, called Turtle Rock, was erected as a monument to the stupidity of war (turtles being regarded in Thailand as none too intelligent). Legend has it that two cities, which once thrived on Phu Rua, went to war over a disagreement concerning a royal marriage. The conflict culminated in an attack on the

wedding procession, during which a bowl, cooking utensils and a cow, which were part of the dowry, were destroyed and magically turned into some of the monoliths that can still be seen in the park to this day.

Animals

Small, isolated and besieged with poachers, the park supports few animals. A few Common Barking Deer, Siamese Hares and several squirrel species are all that remain. The bird list is also relatively short, with only 105 species confirmed at present. There are, however, several species of bulbul, sunbird, flowerpecker and flycatcher to be found in the park.

The Summit

At the summit of Phu Rua, the aroma of pine trees mingles with that of joss sticks burning at a small Buddhist shrine that marks the park's highest point. Several viewpoints and nature trails nearby provide a dramatic panorama of other flat-topped, sandstone mountains, with a patchwork quilt of agricultural fields occupying the broad plains and valleys in between. On especially clear days, the mighty Mekong River can be seen, with Laos stretching away into the distance.

THAP LAN NATIONAL PARK

Restoring the Forest

Established in 1981, Thailand's second-largest and rarely visited national park, Thap Lan, covers an area of 2,235 square kilometres (863 square miles). The park adjoins Pang Sida National Park to the south. The combined areas of the two national parks amount to 3,084 square kilometres (1,190 square miles), making them one of the largest protected areas in the region. With more than 70 per cent forest cover, the park provides a fine refuge for healthy populations of wildlife.

Trees and Forests

Most of the park is covered in evergreen forest, much of it at lower elevations, a habitat all but eliminated in most other areas. A great many Talipot Palm trees grow in some areas of the park. This amazing tree grows for 20–30 years, gradually accumulating energy reserves, before producing a single massive inflorescence, the largest in the plant kingdom, containing millions of flowers. After this stupendous once-in-a-lifetime reproductive effort, the tree dies. Producing such

Above, right: The Talipot Palm (Corypha umbraculifera), after which this park is named, produces the world's largest cluster of flowers (inflorescence).

vast numbers of seeds at one time satiates the animals that eat them, allowing a few seeds to escape their attentions and to grow into new trees. This palm occupies a special place in Thai culture, since its leaves were used as parchment, on which Buddhist texts were inscribed.

Last Hope for the Kouprey?

Thap Lan and Pang Sida provide the last faint hope that the Kouprey may still survive in Thailand. One of the most endangered mammals in the world, this primitive cattle species could provide genes valuable in the production of disease-free strains of domestic cattle. No Kouprey has, however, been observed within Thailand's borders for more than 30 years, and it is extremely unlikely that the species still survives in the country. Elsewhere, less than 100 individuals may still exist in small isolated populations scattered across Cambodia, Laos and Vietnam.

Wildlife

The dense forests of Thap Lan are largely unexplored by zoologists, but at least 76 mammal species have been confirmed within the park, including Pileated Gibbon,

Location: In Nakhon Ratchasima and Prachinburi Provinces, 200 km (125 miles) northeast from Bangkok.

Climate: Monsoonal: average annual temperature 28°C (82°F); average annual rainfall approximately 900 mm (35 in); rainy season May–October (wettest in October, 269 mm/11 in); cool, dry season November–February (coolest in December, 24°C/75°F); hot, dry season March–April (hottest in April, 31°C/88°F).

When to Go: The cool season is the most comfortable time of year for camping and forest treks.

Access: By car, from Bangkok, travel northeast to Nakhon Nayok (Highway 305) and Kabin Buri (Highway 33), then 32 km (20 miles) north on Highway 304, to the park headquarters, east of the main road at Ban Thap Lan. Make arrangements to travel into the park at the park headquarters.

Permits: None required, but contact the Royal Forest Department in Bangkok to arrange your visit.

Equipment: Insect repellent and protection against malaria; camping equipment; light clothes and stout boots for walking; warm clothes in the cool season.

Facilities: Minimal; camping by arrangement; visitors should bring all their own food.

Watching Wildlife: Asian Elephants, Gaur, Pileated Gibbon, deer, civets and possibly Tigers and bears; 149 bird species, including many birds of prey and three hornbill species.

Visitor Activities: Forest walks; reforestation projects; watching birds and mammals.

Right: *The Collared Kingfisher is a common resident along the coast and can be seen inland throughout north-east Thailand.*

Opposite, above: *A serene river glides past the small village of Ban Thai Samakee, where forest restoration efforts are underway. Preservation of water resources provides a strong incentive for local people to become involved in forest restoration.*

Opposite, left: *The Asiatic Jackal usually scavenges for food alone at night. They often enter camp sites or villages to search for left over food.*

Opposite, right: *The Green Dragontail Butterfly prefers dense forest near water and is on the wing from March to June.*

Asiatic Jackal, Smooth Indian Otter, Large-spotted Civet, Fishing Cat, Jungle Cat, Golden Cat, Leopard, Tiger, Asian Elephant, Banteng and Gaur. Totals of 17 amphibian and 39 reptile species have been reported, the latter including the Siamese Crocodile, but it is most unlikely that this species still survives in the park. It may still occur in Vietnam and Cambodia. Confirmed bird species in the national park number 149, including several scarce species restricted to low-land evergreen forest, such as Green Imperial Pigeon, Stork-billed Kingfisher, Jerdon's Baza, and Scaly-crowned Babbler.

Co-operation for Reforestation

Communist guerrillas sought refuge in the area in the 1960s to 1970s, clearing forest for rice cultivation. Remnants of their encampments can still be seen. Later on, influential officials exploited local villagers to carry out illegal logging. The loggers often settled in the park to clear new land for agriculture. Recently, however, attitudes have begun to change, and the villagers themselves are collaborating with park authorities to restore the park's forest.

At one such project, near Ban Thai Samakee in Amphur Wang Nam Kieou, the Petroleum Authority of Thailand has sponsored tree planting at the edge of the park. The trees are provided by the Royal Forest Department and are planted by local villagers as part of a nation-wide effort to reforest 8,000 square kilometres (3,000 square miles) of degraded land, to celebrate the King's Golden Jubilee. Wildlife Fund Thailand (WFT), one of Thailand's leading non-governmental conservation organizations, provides expertise and training for the villagers, and has helped them to make an exhibition in the village to explain the project to the general public. There is even a nature trail along which guides from the village lead educational groups through the planted sites, as well as some of the remaining patches of original forest. Since tree planting began and hunting stopped, large animals have returned to the area. The nature trail is dotted with the tracks of Asian Elephant, Sambar Deer, Common Barking Deer, Common Wild Pig and Gaur. Tigers, Asian Wild Dogs and Asiatic Black Bears have all been seen in the area. The project has produced a nature trail guidebook to help walkers identify the tracks.

SOUTHERN THAILAND

Dramatic coastal scenery, coral reefs and verdant forests draw millions of tourists to southern Thailand every year. Limestone karst, sculptured by wind and water, is the dominant scenic feature, towering above both coastal and forest habitats. Caves along the Ao Phangnga coast sheltered Thailand's earliest human inhabitants, Hoabinhians, who lived amongst primeval rainforest more than 40,000 years ago.

In the Andaman Sea, Tarutao is Southeast Asia's largest marine reserve, with coral reefs and nesting beaches for sea turtles. Farther north, Mu Ko Surin Marine National Park is Thailand's finest coral-diving site.

Such natural beauty is bound to attract the entrepreneurs that cater for tourists. Mu Ko Phi Phi is a park tainted by tourism. Although the area retains magnificent scenery, coral reefs and seabirds, it has suffered greatly from overdevelopment. Sirinath Marine National Park, on the popular island of Phuket, is also threatened, but villagers protect the nesting beaches of sea turtles, and the easily accessible coral reef provides an excellent introduction to this delicate marine ecosystem.

Off the east coast of the southern peninsula, the tiny limestone islands of Mu Ko Ang Thong Marine National Park have escaped the worst depredations of the tourism industry.

Southern Thailand provides unique recreational opportunities. Krabi is a challenging destination for rock climbers, whilst sea canoeing provides an ecologically friendly way to explore mangrove forests and sea caves.

Forests here have an equatorial atmosphere and are home to several endemic plants. Khao Sok features giant *Rafflesia* flowers and unique palms, whilst Thaleban combines the attractions of lush evergreen forest with coastal mangroves.

HAD NOPPARAT THARA– MU KO PHI PHI MARINE NATIONAL PARK

Spectacular Tropical Island Scenery

Travellers seeking a tropical paradise need look no farther than Ko Phi Phi with its sheer forested, limestone cliffs rising 300 metres (984 feet) from a turquoise sea, interspersed with pristine white sandy bays and colourful coral reefs just off-shore. Little wonder then that the park was chosen as the setting for the Hollywood blockbuster, *The Beach*.

The Phi Phi island group lies in the Andaman Sea, midway between Thailand's largest island, Phuket, and the coast of Krabi Province. Established in 1983, the park extends north to include

Opposite, left above: *Swimming and snorkelling around the coral reefs are the most popular activities at Ko Phi Phi.*

Opposite, left centre: *White-bellied Sea-eagles can be seen soaring around Ko Phi Phi's mighty cliffs.*

Opposite, left below: *Nudibranches, or sea slugs, come in many colours.*

Opposite, right: *Rising and falling tides and wave action undercut the bases of limestone karst outcrops, creating rocky overhangs and caves.*

Above, right: *Lohdalam Bay from a viewpoint on Ko Phi Phi Don.*

Previous pages:
Page 132: *A sweeping bay near Chumphon.* Page 133: *Agloaonema simplex is a common succulent ground herb.*

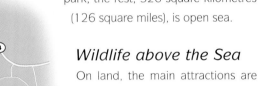

some of Krabi's finest mainland beaches, ranked amongst the most beautiful in the world. Land comprises only 64 square kilometres (25 square miles) of the park; the rest, 326 square kilometres (126 square miles), is open sea.

Wildlife above the Sea

On land, the main attractions are coastal birds and some of the remarkable plants that cling to existence by rooting in the crevices of the limestone cliffs. One such plant is *Euphorbia antiquorum*, which resembles a cactus, with its expandable, succulent green stems, star-shaped in cross-section. The thick stems not only carry out photosynthesis, but also store water for use in the dry season. Shortage of water makes the limestone crags a very challenging environment for plants.

Seabirds

Although the number of confirmed bird species in the national park is comparatively low (only 66), the bird list does include some notable rarities. All three frigatebird species (Christmas, Great and Lesser) known from Thailand have been recorded in the national park. Although they do not breed in Thailand, they do occur as uncommon winter visitors, and can sometimes be seen stealing food from other seabirds in daring mid-air attacks. The park is host to no fewer than six tern species, four of

Location: In the Andaman Sea, south off the coast of Krabi Province.

Climate: Average annual temperature 28°C (82°F); annual rainfall 1,900 mm (75 in); wettest in September (400 mm/16 in); hottest in March, coolest in November.

When to Go: December–April. The southwest monsoon May–November brings unpredictable weather and choppy seas. Boats will, however, run from Phuket and Krabi whenever sea conditions permit.

Access: Regular boat services from Phuket or the pier in Krabi City. Many tour agencies run day trips to Ko Phi Phi, including the main scenic highlights, swimming or diving and lunch. Alternatively boats can be chartered for personalized itineraries.

Permits: None required.

Equipment: Sunblock, insect repellent; swimming gear; snorkelling gear.

Facilities: A wide range of resort-style accommodation, operated by the private sector, is available on Ko Phi Phi Don and can be booked through travel agents; campsites; visitor centre; diving centres.

Watching Wildlife: Seabirds, raptors, swiftlets; limestone plants; corals, fish and other marine animals.

Visitor Activities: Swimming, birdwatching; snorkelling and scuba diving.

Right: *Plenty of local boats are available to ferry visitors between the bays and beaches.*

Below: *Common Lettuce Coral is found in shallow reefs up to a depth of 15 metres (50 feet).*

which (Roseate, Black-naped, Bridled and Great Crested) are ranked as endangered. They nest on some of the more remote, small, rocky islets and beaches, well away from disturbance.

Raptors

The craggy limestone cliffs that create such a magnificent frame to the park's beaches also provide niches where raptors, including White-bellied Sea-eagles, Brahminy Kites and Peregrine Falcons, build their nest platforms. In addition, the cliffs provide Peregrine Falcons with perfect vantage points from which to launch deadly dives down onto their prey, often pigeons or small seabirds, during which the falcons achieve speeds which rank them amongst the fastest birds on Earth.

Bird's-nest Soup

Several caves around the Phi Phi islands support colonies of Edible-nest Swiftlets, the most famous of which is the inappropriately named Viking Cave (the Vikings were never there). Today, the thousands of visitors who arrive daily to view rock paintings in Viking Cave have driven away most of the birds, but the species still survives in less-disturbed nooks along the coastal cliffs. The swiftlets make tiny, white, cup-shaped nests from saliva, the principle ingredient of bird's-nest soup, a very expensive delicacy in Chinese cuisine. The nests can sell for up to £1,500 (US$ 2,250) per kilogram. Collectors lease the right to harvest the nests at each site, climbing up precarious bamboo scaffolding to reach the highest recesses where the birds build their nests. It is not uncommon for a nest collector to fall to his death.

Apart from bats, very few mammals live on the islands. Lesser Mouse Deer, Common Wild Pig, Long-tailed Macaque and Grey-bellied Squirrel have, however, been recorded.

Right: *Viking Cave is famous for its cave paintings, mostly of ships, of various ages. This depiction of a Chinese junk is probably about 200 years old.*

Wildlife below the Sea

The best sites for snorkellers and scuba divers lie to the south or west of Phi Phi Don and Phi Phi Ley. Maya Bay provides an ideal shallow reef for snorkelling. Eight kilometres (5 miles) west of Phi Phi Ley there is a small rocky outcrop known as Shark Point, with submerged pinnacles, a rock arch adorned with soft corals and crystal-clear waters. The main attraction to scuba divers there is the abundance of Leopard Sharks, up to 2 metres (6½ feet) in length, usually found resting on the seabed. Cuttlefish, gathering for breeding, sea whips, moray eels and several species of spiny lobster are just a few of the many marine delights that await divers around the Phi Phi islands.

Trouble in Paradise

In such an idyllic location, it is a great shame that mass-tourism development could not be prevented. Entirely inappropriate hotel construction and sprawling bungalows, in enclaves excluded from the national park, have created eyesores on Phi Phi Don. Muslim and Sea Gypsy communities, established before the islands became a national park, have expanded, causing squalor. Although the scenic grandeur of these islands remains largely intact, damage to coral reefs due to pollution, boat anchors and overuse by tourists has significantly reduced the amount of living coral in the national park.

'The Beach'

Use of the park as the set of the movie *The Beach* enraged local environmentalists. Beach vegetation was disturbed as the Hollywood crew attempted to remodel one of the bays, but they also cleared away several tons of long-accumulated garbage. The ethics of using a national park to generate revenue for a foreign movie company was one of the questions raised by the environmentalists. In reality, however, the short-term disturbance caused by the movie pales into insignificance compared with the massive, blatant, on-going destruction being wrought by greedy, local tourism developers. Surprisingly, it is probably the bird's-nest collectors that have done most to limit the ravages of the tourism industry around Ko Phi Phi, since they jealously guard their concessions against encroachment.

Below: Sea fans are found in sub-tidal reefs. The coral polyps feed on zooplankton, mostly at night.

Below, left: Long-spined Sea Urchins are abundant throughout the Gulf and Andaman Sea on coral reefs and rocky shores.

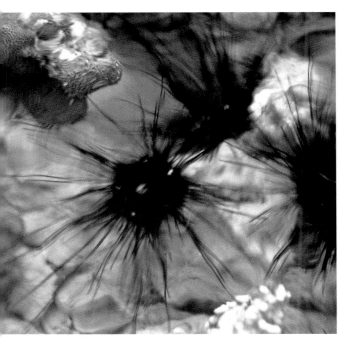

KHAO SOK NATIONAL PARK

Giant Rafflesia Flowers

Established in 1980, Khao Sok National Park conserves 739 square kilometres (285 square miles) of forested hills in Surat Thani Province. It is the heart of an expansive complex of five contiguous conservation sites that comprise the largest protected forest on the Thai–Malay peninsula. The park consists of mudstone or siltstone hills, punctuated by towering outcrops of limestone karst, rising to 960 metres (3,150 feet). Situated in one of the wettest areas of Thailand, Khao Sok's forest displays an exuberance normally associated with tropical rainforest. Its most famous botanical treasure, *Rafflesia kerrii*, which produces one of the largest flowers in the world, represents a family more typical of equatorial rainforest.

Botanical Treasures

In the 1920s, A. F. G. Kerr, Thailand's first Government botanist, was appointed to survey the Kingdom's plant resources. In southern Thailand, he collected a giant *Rafflesia* flower, mistakenly labelling it as a species already described from Malaysia. It was not until the 1980s, when botanist Willem Meijer re-examined Kerr's dried specimens, that the species was recognized as new to science. Further exploration at Khao Sok eventually led to rediscovery of the living plant.

The flowers of *Rafflesia kerrii* (in Thai *buah poot* or *buah toom*) are undoubtedly the largest, most magnificent and most bizarre in Thailand. Like all members of the Rafflesiaceae, this species is parasitic, possessing no green leaves. For most of the year, it exists as microscopic filaments growing inside the roots of lianas of the grape family. Occasionally, however, the plant develops buds which burst through the bark of the host's roots, grow to the size of a cabbage, eventually

Opposite, above:
Towering limestone cliffs densely clad in evergreen forest are the main scenic feature of this national park.

Opposite, below left: Zingiber spectabile, *one of many ginger species common in Thailand's evergreen forests.*

Opposite, below right: *Naturalist Dr Hans Banziger, from Chiang Mai University, examines Thailand's largest flower,* Rafflesia kerrii, *for the carrion flies which pollinate it.*

Above, right: *White-throated Kingfisher, one of seven species confirmed for this national park. This species is a common resident in open woodlands throughout the country.*

Location: Surat Thani Province, 70 km (44 miles) southwest of the provincial capital.

Climate: Heavy monsoonal rains for 9–10 months each year, with a short dry spell from December to early February; average annual rainfall exceeds 3,500 mm (138 in); hot and humid all year.

When to Go: For the most comfortable weather and the chance of seeing *Rafflesia* flowers, visit from November to early February.

Access: Follow Highway 401 from Surat Thani or Takua Pa to Km 109, where a narrow road leads north 1.5 km (1 mile) to the park headquarters. Public buses stop near the headquarters. The reservoir is also reached from Highway 401, via a narrow road running north from Ban Takum, Km 52–53.

Permits: None required.

Equipment: Protection against insects and leeches, and wet-weather gear essential; light clothes and tough footwear for forest treks; a torch for caves.

Facilities: At the park headquarters, houses for rent and campsite; a visitor centre with exhibition and self-guided trails; raft houses at the dam and bungalows at Chiew Larn substation; boats for charter on the reservoir. Private-sector resorts near the park headquarters.

Watching Wildlife: *Rafflesia* flowers and palms; Asian Elephants, deer, Serows, gibbons and monkeys, flying squirrels; raptors and hornbills.

Visitor Activities: Forest walks and nature trails; watching wildlife; visiting waterfalls and caves; viewing rare plants; boating on reservoir.

Map labels: To Ranong; Suk Samaran; Si Phangnga National Park; THAILAND; Bangkok; Khuraburi; Tam Nang; Chiew Larn Dam; Khao Sok National Park; Park Headquarters; To Surat Thani; Takuapa; Phanom; Thung Biri; To Phuket

Right: *The rare and beautiful palm* Kerriodoxa elegans *grows only in Khao Sok National Park and on Phuket Island.*

Below: *Khao Sok's caves provide roosting sites for vast numbers of bats. Their mass exit at dusk is a wildlife spectacle not to be missed.*

opening into flowers 70 centimetres (28 inches) or more in diameter, lasting just a few days during December and January.

Dr Hans Banziger of Chiang Mai University studied the extraordinary pollination system of this species, which has separate male and female flowers. Carrion flies are attracted to the male flowers by their foul stench, which resembles rotting flesh. They are then lured inside the flower's gaping cavity by a fruity fragrance within, which falsely appears to promise sugars. Channels inside the flower manipulate the flies towards the anthers, where mushy pollen is deposited on the flies' backs. This process is repeated when flies daubed with pollen mush visit female flowers, except that the flies are manipulated into spreading their pollen load onto the flower's stigma. As for seed dispersal, no direct observations have been made. Many creatures, ranging in size from ants to elephants, have been suggested as seed dispersers.

Other botanical specialities of the park include palms. *Kerriodoxa elegans*, which has beautiful fan-shaped leaves with a silvery underside, grows only at Khao Sok and on Phuket. The recently discovered *Maxburrettia furtadoana*, endemic to southern Thailand, flourishes around the Chiew Larn Reservoir.

Animals

A total of 48 mammal species has been recorded within the national park, including Asian Elephant, Leopard, Banteng, Gaur, Dusky Langur, White-handed Gibbon, Malayan Tapir and Malayan Sun Bear. Perhaps fewer than 10 Tigers now survive in Khao Sok. Poaching, to provide products for bogus folk medicines, has caused their decline. Serow, a black, goat-like antelope, retreats to the limestone crags to avoid predation by Leopards or Tigers. Today, however, human beings are their greatest predator. They are killed for scent glands below their eyes, used in Chinese medicine. Vast numbers of bats roost within the park's many caves, particularly the appropriately named Bat Cave (Tum Kang Kao), near Klong Pae checkpoint. At least 38 bat species have been confirmed within the park.

Among the 188 bird species recorded in the park, rare raptors include Bat Hawk, Lesser Fish-eagle and Wallace's Hawk Eagle. Seven kingfisher species, five hornbill species and 12 woodpecker species are among the park's more flamboyant birds.

Chiew Larn Reservoir — Animal Rescue

Shortly after Khao Sok was declared a national park, the Electricity Generating Authority of Thailand (EGAT) began constructing the 95-metre (312-foot) high Rachabrapah Dam across the Pasaeng River, creating the 165-square-kilometre (64-square-mile) Chiew Larn Reservoir. The dam was a catastrophe for local wildlife.

A much publicized wildlife rescue operation, funded by EGAT and led by one of Thailand's most inspirational conservationists, the late Seub Nakhasathien, saved many animals from drowning. Rescued animals, including monkeys, Serows, deer, snakes and lizards, were relocated to higher ground and some were monitored after release, using radio collars, to discover how they adjusted to their new habitats. Although much knowledge was gained from this project, the effects were largely cosmetic. Many animals died during the rescue attempt and even those successfully relocated could not establish territories amongst the crowded wildlife populations fleeing the rising waters. The wildlife rescue operation could not compensate for the loss of critical lowland, riverine rainforest, and several species have never recovered from the disaster.

One probable casualty of the dam was the exceedingly rare Storm's Stork. In 1986 a nesting pair was observed, for the first time in Thailand, along a tributary of the Pasang River. Later, another nest was observed in a tall dipterocarp tree above the rising waters of the reservoir but, since then, no more have been seen.

Today, the reservoir provides a fabulous recreational opportunity to visitors. Limestone cliffs tower more than 900 metres (2,950 feet) above the reservoir's surface, nearly three times taller than the famous formations in Phangnga Bay. Hired boats and simple accommodation allow visitors to explore the convoluted shoreline. Gibbons, monkeys, raptors, hornbills, Common Flying Foxes and large monitor lizards are commonly seen in the near-vertical forest that surrounds the lake, whilst Asian Elephants and Tigers visit the shoreline very occasionally.

Left: *The shape and colour of many insects attempt mimicry or camouflage, but the extraordinary form of this insect (Fulgoridae) leaves the observer mystified.*

Left: *Still waters reflect extraordinary limestone formations shrouded in mist; a captivating scene on the Chiew Larn Reservoir.*

Ao Phangnga Marine National Park and Krabi

Dramatic Karst Scenery

Location: The western and southern coastline between the provincial capitals of Krabi and Phangnga Provinces.

Climate: Average annual temperature 23°C (73°F); average annual rainfall 2,380 mm (94 in); hottest in May–April; coolest in November–February; rainy season May–October.

When to Go: Phangnga Bay is sheltered and calm all year around, but the best time to visit is November to May.

Access: By organized tours or rented cars and boats from the tourism centres of Krabi and Phuket. Thai Airways flies to both Phuket and Krabi.

Permits: None required.

Equipment: Protection against the sun is essential when travelling by boat; insect repellent; snorkelling or scuba gear; rock-climbing equipment.

Facilities: A wide range of accommodation and restaurants in the town of Krabi, the resort beaches of Phuket and at Laem Phra Nang; simple guesthouses in the town of Phangnga; Forest Department bungalows at Phangnga and Had Nopparat Thara; organized tours and boats for charter from Krabi and Phuket resort beaches.

Watching Wildlife: Monkeys, flying foxes, seabirds and dolphins.

Visitor Activities: Birdwatching; boat trips and sea canoeing; visiting caves; rock climbing; snorkelling and scuba diving.

A highly fragmented spine of limestone runs down the western side of Thailand. This limestone formed during the Permian Period, 225–280 million years ago, as shellfish and corals accumulated in a shallow sea along a barrier reef that stretched from southern China to Borneo. For millions of years, the limestone was buried and compressed beneath younger sediments, but 3–60 million years ago India collided with the rest of Asia, thrusting up the Himalayas as well as a tail of lower hills running down Thailand's western border with Myanmar. The long-buried layers of Permian limestone were fractured and exposed, then eroded by monsoonal rains. Plant roots cracked open the rock, and acid from decomposing humus dissolved the limestone, widening the cracks. Water, seeping through the fractured rock, formed underground streams and vast cave systems. Along the coast, fluctuating sea levels and wave movement sculptured the limestone into a bewildering array of formations. This breathtaking seascape is termed drowned karstland by geologists and reaches its zenith in Phangnga Bay.

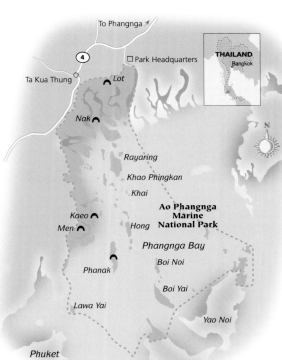

Opposite: Towering limestone cliffs, densely clad in luxuriant vegetation and eroded by wind and waves into extraordinary formations, are the dominant scenic features.

Above, right: Surgeonfish are so-named because they bear sharp spines on either side of the tail, which may be used to inflict wounds on enemies.

Ao Phangnga Marine National Park

Phangnga Bay presents a landscape of immense limestone crags, set amidst mangrove forest in a shallow sea, which is barely one metre deep in places. The bay was declared a marine national park in 1981. It covers 40 sculptured islands, totalling 53 square kilometres (20 square miles), and 347 square kilometres (134 square miles) of cloudy, turquoise ocean. The craggy cliffs, rising to a height of up to 400 metres (1,312 feet), are often pockmarked with gaping cave entrances. Rock paintings, dating back at least 3,000 years, that depict crocodiles, dolphins, sharks and people have been found at Khao Khian, near the mouth of the Phangnga River.

Sea Canoes

Most tourist boats head straight for 'James Bond Island', the famous setting for the film, *The Man with the Golden Gun*. Another busy attraction is the so-called 'Sea Gypsy Village' (the community is actually Muslim, not Sea Gypsy), comprising approximately 500 houses on stilts around Koh Panyi. A gentler way to see the national park, however, is to book a trip with one of many tour companies now offering travel by sea canoe. Canoes allow access to partially submerged cave passages and massive, hidden, collapsed caverns, known as *hongs*, inside the islands. Some *hongs* contain secret lagoons, whilst others support tiny patches of forest.

The water is too turbid to support corals. A few Dugongs may still occur in the marine park and dolphins are sometimes seen. At least 96 bird species have been recorded, including several rare or endangered species such as Malaysian Plover, Asian Dowitcher, Buffy Fish-owl and Dark-throated Oriole. Amongst the trees that cling to the cliff faces, Common Flying Foxes roost, setting forth at dusk to forage for fruit. Amongst the mangroves, Smooth Indian Otters chase fish, whilst the carnivorous frog *Rana cancrivora* feasts on fiddler crabs.

Plants

Plants that gain a tenuous roothold in the cracks and crevices of the limestone crags face a difficult life. They are exposed to extreme temperature fluctuations and

Above: *Although Railay Beach is situated on the mainland, it is accessible only by boat from Krabi town. It is widely regarded as one of the most beautiful beaches in the world.*

Right: *Growing up to 35 centimetres (14 inches) across, the Blue Sea Star* (Linkia laevigata) *is a common inhabitant of Andaman Sea reefs.*

the full force of monsoonal deluges but, as soon as the rain stops, water rapidly drains away through cracks in the rock, leaving the plants in almost continuous drought conditions. With heat reflected from the light-coloured rock, daytime temperatures soar, threatening plants with desiccation.

However, fortunately many plant species have evolved the means to conserve water and survive in these harsh conditions, including the cycad *Cycas rumphii*, a relic from the age of dinosaurs, with its tough palm-like leaves, deep roots and convoluted woody stem, capable of storing large quantities of water. The palm *Maxburretia furtadiana*, recently discovered by botanists, is endemic to the limestone karst of southern Thailand. With beautiful, fan-shaped leaves, this unique palm can grow to a height of up to 5 metres (16 feet), and roots directly into cracks in the limestone.

Krabi

Approximately 90 kilometres (56 miles) south of Phangnga, Krabi is a charming fishing town, which takes its name from an ancient, legendary sword, or *krabi*, purportedly discovered nearby. Mangroves in the Krabi River estuary provide interesting boat trips for bird-watchers. Mangrove Pitta, Masked Finfoot, Mangrove Blue Flycatcher, Nordmann's Greenshank and five species of kingfisher are just some of the many birds that can be seen.

Above: *The Hill Myna can be seen in forests through-out Thailand. It has the ability to mimic the human voice and for this reason is often kept in captivity.*

Left: *Many tour companies in Krabi now offer sea canoeing as a more eco-logically friendly alterna-tive to conventional boat tours for exploring the mangroves and caves.*

Above: *The dominant geological feature of the Krabi–Phangnga coastline is what geologists call drowned karstland; dramatic pinnacles of limestone plunging into an azure sea.*

Above, right: *These fantastic limestone formations are formed by the constant percolation of rainwater through the limestone and fluctuating sea levels over many thousands of years.*

Opposite: *Long-tailed Macaques, one of six primate species confirmed present in Ao Phangnga Marine National Park. Grooming serves the practical function of removing irritating parasites from the fur.*

The main attractions of Krabi are reached by boat from the town's main pier. Laem Phra Nang (the mainland part of Had Nopparat Thara–Mu Ko Phi Phi Marine National Park) is a limestone headland so rugged that it is completely inaccessible by road. Awesome, sheer cliffs 250 metres (820 feet) high provide a dramatic backdrop to the beaches of Railay and Phra Nang, ranked amongst the five most beautiful in the world. Enclosed and sunken in the heart of the cave is the remarkable Princess Pool, a classic marine *hong*, which fills with seawater, via an underground passage at high tide.

Long-tailed Macaques, one of the most visible mammals on limestone karst, are common around Laem Phra Nang. On forested crags, these monkeys eat small animals and fruits, especially figs that readily root in limestone cracks, whilst down by the sea they forage for crabs and other marine animals.

Caves are prominent features of karstland. Not only are the caves of Krabi richly adorned with stalagmites and stalactites, but several also contain archaeological evidence of the earliest human beings to live in Thailand. Stone tools and hearths, belonging to the ancient Hoabinhians, dated at 43,000 years old, were found a few kilometres north of Krabi town in 1982. Younger,

Stone Age cave paintings, tools, jewellery and human remains have been found in several other caves, particularly in and around Thaan Bok Koranee National Park, 42 kilometres (26 miles) north of the town of Krabi. Established in 1998, this 104-square kilometre (40-square-mile) national park includes nine caves, several accessible only by boat, and a botanical garden. Small waterfalls, cascading into emerald-green pools, create a fairy-tale landscape which attracts hundreds of picnickers at weekends.

Rock Climbing

The area around Krabi and Phangnga is fast becoming one of Southeast Asia's premier rock-climbing sites. A tourist magazine recently described it thus '...for the world's rock climbers, Krabi is not just a Mecca; for them, it's as if the cornucopia of routes on offer up the many sheer walls rising up out of Phangnga Bay and around mean they've died and gone to mountaineering heaven.' Since the mid-1990s there has been a phenomenal increase in this sport, particularly around Laem Phra Nang, where 300 climbing routes have been pioneered. Any of the bungalow resorts at Laem Phra Nang can provide rock-climbing instructors and guides.

Mu Ko Surin Marine National Park

Thailand's Premier Coral Dive Site

Mu Ko Surin Marine National Park is one of Thailand's finest dive sites and the most popular destination for live-aboard diving tours. The coral reefs of this park present a kaleidoscope of living colour, whilst the opportunity to swim with Manta Rays, sea turtles and Whale Sharks provide snorkellers and divers with the ultimate tropical marine experience.

Established in 1981 in the Andaman Sea, west of the small town of Khuraburi, this superb marine park protects five granite islands and their fringing coral reefs, considered to be amongst the most beautiful in Thailand's waters. The park has an area of 135 square kilometres (52 square miles), 76 per cent of which is made up of sea.

Opposite, top: *Largest of their kind, Manta Rays gliding through the ocean feeding on plankton are one of the top marine attractions of this famous diving site.*

Opposite, below: *The gentle Whale Shark is the world's biggest fish species. It is not dangerous to human beings, preferring smaller prey such as plankton and small fish.*

Above, right: *The Nicobar Pigeon is instantly distinguished from other pigeons by the shaggy plumage around its neck. It is a very rare resident in evergreen forest on just a few islands in the Andaman Sea.*

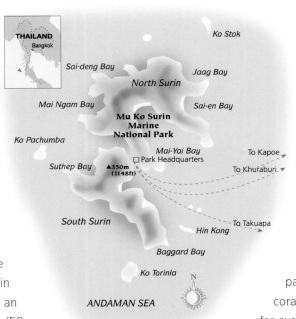

Marine Highlights

No other ecosystem matches the colour and diversity of coral reefs. With an evolutionary history that stretches back longer than any other ecosystem, coral reefs support some of the most ancient species, as well as the most highly developed of ecological inter-relationships. The Surin Islands showcase a variety of different coral-reef environments, from simple fringing reefs to multilevel reefs, plunging vertical walls and underwater pinnacles. The park supports at least 200 coral species, providing habitat for over 800 species of fish.

Ko Tachai, with its three-tiered reef, 12 to 22 metres (39 to 72 feet) deep, provides an excellent introduction to the colourful world of coral. Staghorn corals, brain corals, mushroom corals and fire corals, along with multi-coloured soft corals and ruby-red gorgonian sea fans, provide the basic framework of the ecosystem. All are comprised of colonies of polyps requiring clear warm water for their survival. Amongst the hard corals, giant clams live by filtering food from seawater and absorbing nutriment from single-celled algae (zooxanthellae), that live within this bivalve's mantle and are responsible for its brilliant turquoise colour. Butterfly fish, angel fish, lion fish and puffer fish swim around the reef, whilst Moray

Map labels

THAILAND
Bangkok

Ko Stok
Sai-deng Bay
Jaag Bay
North Surin
Sai-en Bay
Mai Ngam Bay
Mu Ko Surin Marine National Park
Ko Pachumba
Mai-Yai Bay
Park Headquarters
To Kapoe
Suthep Bay
▲350m (1148ft)
To Khuraburi
South Surin
Hin Kong
To Takuapa
Baggard Bay
Ko Torinla
ANDAMAN SEA

Location: In the Andaman Sea, part of Phangnga Province, approximately 70 km (44 miles) west of Khuraburi.

Climate: Southwest monsoon, May–November, causes rough seas; average annual temperature 28°C (82°F); average rainfall approximately 4,000 mm (158 in); wettest in September (500 mm/20 in); dry and pleasant December–April; hottest in March (34°C/93°F), coolest in November (24°C/75°F).

When to Go: From December to April.

Access: By four-hour boat trip from Ban Hin Lat, 4 km (2½ miles) west of Km 110 on Highway 4. This turnoff is 70 km (44 miles) south of Ranong. Organized dive tours from Phuket, lasting up to a week.

Permits: None required. An entrance fee is charged. Contact the park office by telephone (076 491378) to arrange your visit.

Equipment: Sunblock and protection against insects are essential; swimming, snorkelling and scuba gear and a lifejacket.

Facilities: A mainland office at Ban Hin Lat; live-on-board diving tours, mostly booked in Phuket. The park operates long-tailed boats to the main snorkelling sites and rents out equipment and lifejackets. A restaurant, dormitory accommodation and campsite on Ko Surin Nua; forest and marine nature trails and exhibition.

Watching Wildlife: Whale Sharks, Manta Rays, sea turtles, coral reefs, anemones and their associated fish, rock lobsters; sea birds, pigeons and raptors.

Visitor Activities: Swimming, snorkelling and scuba diving; birdwatching and forest walks.

Right: *A local fishing boat moored near one of the park's beaches. Sanctuaries, such as Ko Surin protect the breeding grounds of many fish species that will later be caught by the fishing industry.*

Eels, rock lobsters and a wide range of other crustaceans shelter in the crevices. Barracuda and sailfish cruise near the surface.

Largest of Their Kind

Ko Bon is the place to try your luck at spotting Manta Rays and Whale Sharks, both occasional visitors to these waters. The Whale Shark is the biggest fish in the world, growing up to 15 metres (50 feet) long. It is dark-blue above and white below, with white spots and lines.

Along the head and back are several broad longitudinal ridges. Surprisingly, this gentle giant subsists on the ocean's smallest creatures, filtering plankton and small fish from the seawater. Manta Rays, the largest rays in the world, also cruise the depths filtering plankton. Their massive 'wingspan' reaches up to 6 metres (nearly 20 feet), and they can weigh up to 1,600 kilograms (1 1/2 tons).

Four species of sea turtle occur within the park, including the world's largest species, the Leatherback, with a skin-covered carapace up to 1.8 metres (6 feet) in length. These giants paddle over vast distances, feeding on jellyfish, but return to sandy beaches to lay their eggs. The females dig a nest hole about one metre deep and lay up to 140 eggs before returning to the sea. When the eggs hatch, the young fend for themselves, heading straight for the sea, to find security amongst the coral reefs until they grow big enough to be safe from predators. The three other species of sea turtle around the Surin Islands are Hawksbill, Olive Ridley and Green. Ao Tau, on South Surin Island, is a good place to look for them.

Off Suthep Bay, an underwater nature trail has been established by eminent marine biologist Dr Thon Thamrongnawasawat. The 100-metre (328-foot) trail, marked with numbered buoys, displays corals, anemone fish, sponges and giant clams. Information along the trail is provided in a waterproof brochure.

Below: *This Feather-finned Butterfly Fish* (Heniochus acuminatus) *is usually solitary and is found in sub-tidal reefs in both the Andaman Sea and the Gulf of Thailand.*

Tropical Rainforest

Although marine ecosystems are the main attraction of Ko Surin, the forests are also worth visiting since they are amongst the few true tropical rainforests in Thailand, with annual rainfall exceeding 4,000 millimetres (158 inches). The trail from the campsite to Mai Ngam Bay provides an excellent introduction to the islands' forests. Near the coast, massive *Pterocymbium tinctorium* and *Pterygota alata* trees provide the main canopy, up to 35 metres (115 feet) high, with *Dracontolmelon mangiferum*, *Swintonia griffithii*, *Parishia insignis* and dipterocarps taking over higher up. Rattan palms, other lianas, strangling figs, ferns, vines, creepers and a host of epiphytes add structural diversity. These evergreen forests are habitat for one of Thailand's rarest pigeons. The Nicobar Pigeon, with its distinctive ruff of iridescent bronze neck hackles, lives only in evergreen forest on the most undisturbed islands in the Andaman Sea. Amongst the undergrowth, Lesser Mouse Deer can sometimes be seen, whilst flying foxes roost in trees overhead. Flying Lemur, Pig-tailed Macaques, Reticulated Python and monitor lizards have all been recorded.

Birds

At least 88 bird species have been recorded in the park. Notable raptors include White-bellied Sea-eagle, Brahminy Kite, Chinese Goshawk and Peregrine Falcon. Over the ocean, Short-tailed Shearwater has been recorded, as well as five tern species. In the forest, in addition to the Nicobar Pigeon, six other pigeon species occur, including Pied Imperial and Green Imperial, as well as Wreathed Hornbill and Ruddy Kingfisher.

Above: *Giant clams are fairly common amongst the reefs around the Islands.*

Left: *Staghorn corals are one of the basic building blocks of reefs in shallow waters and inter-tidal zones.*

Below: *A young Hawksbill Sea Turtle finds food and security amongst the coral.*

MU KO ANG THONG MARINE NATIONAL PARK

Secret Lagoon and Marine Life

Situated 30 kilometres (19 miles) off the popular resort island of Samui, Ang Thong Marine National Park provides an ideal day-trip for tourists to view some of the most attractive oceanic scenery in the Gulf of Thailand. The park was established in 1980 and its name means 'Golden Bowl'. It comprises a compact archipelago of 42 tiny islands, with a combined area of only 18 square kilometres (7 square miles) and 84 square kilometres (32 square miles) of shallow open sea. The islands are steep-sided outcrops of limestone, rising to 400 metres (1,312 feet), eroded by the waves into sculptured formations, and covered in dense evergreen and mixed deciduous forest. Secluded bays have beaches with pristine white sand for swimming or relaxing, whilst offshore there are coral reefs for snorkellers to explore.

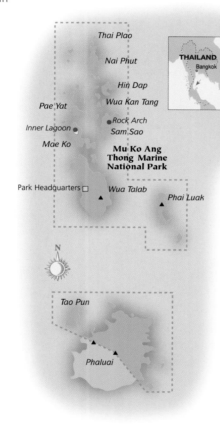

Opposite: *Sheer limestone cliffs smothered in exotic vegetation, including cycads and* Euphorbia antiquorum, *are typical of Ang Thong National Park.*

Above, right: *Triangle-tailed Horse-shoe Crabs inhabit subtidal areas and congregate on sandy beaches for mating from April until December.*

The Sea Within

The greatest attraction of the park is the salt-water lagoon called Thale Nai ('Inner Sea'), entirely surrounded by sheer cliffs, in the centre of Mae Ko. The roughly circular lagoon, approximately 250 metres (820 feet) in diameter, was probably formed when the roof of a huge cavern collapsed. Shallow, turquoise seawater, teeming with fish, now fills the void, providing a highly photogenic geological feature. The lagoon is a 15-minute boat ride from the park headquarters, followed by a steep climb up and over the 'crater' wall. Another interesting geological feature of the park is a distinctive rock arch off Sam Sao Island.

Around the cliffs, Brahminy Kites and White-bellied Sea-eagles soar on thermals. Inside caves along the coastline, Edible-nest Swiftlets provide a lucrative harvest for those brave enough to scale the cave walls to collect the nests, which are the principle ingredient of the expensive Chinese delicacy, bird's-nest soup. Dolphins are occasionally spotted on boat trips through the park.

Coral Reefs

Corals are not extensive in the park, being limited by sediment and freshwater pouring into the Gulf from the Tapi Phumduang and other rivers draining the mainland.

Location: 70 km (44 miles) northeast of Surat Thani in the Gulf of Thailand.

Climate: Very rainy during the northeast monsoon (October–February) and the southwest monsoon (May–September); drier and sunny February–April: average annual rainfall 2,000 mm (79 in), average annual temperature 23°C (73°F).

When to Go: February–May. At other times of the year, winds during the monsoon periods cause rough seas and turbid water.

Access: By boat from Surat Thani or from Na Thon on Ko Samui. Most local travel agents run day tours that include the boat trip, lunch and snorkelling equipment.

Permits: None required. Arrange your trip by contacting the park headquarters in Surat Thani (telephone: 077-283025).

Equipment: For the beaches and reefs, sunblock and snorkelling equipment; for jungle walks, light clothes, strong boots and insect repellent.

Facilities: At Wua Ta Lap, bungalows, camping, a small information centre and restaurant, local boats for hire.

Watching Wildlife: Coastal birds, common corals and reef fish, dolphins.

Visitor Activities: Boat trips, swimming and snorkelling, jungle walks and birdwatching.

Right: Often mistaken as a cactus, Euphorbia antiquorum *has spiny angular stems which carry out photosynthesis and store water.*

Below: A slow mover, the Blacktip or Red-Barred Grouper excels to great speeds when attacking prey.

Bottom: Although the reefs around Ang Thong cannot be compared with those of the Andaman Sea, there are still sufficient sea fans and corals to interest divers and snorkellers.

They occur mostly as narrow fringing reefs close to the beaches, especially in sheltered areas along the southwestern or northeastern shores of the islands. Some of the best sites for snorkellers are around the islands of Sam Sao, Thai Plao and Wua Kan Tang. Inshore, brain coral, hump corals (e.g. *Porites lutea*), and staghorn corals (*Acropora*) are common, whilst in deeper waters leaf corals (*Pavona*) and flower or anemone corals (e.g. *Goniopora djibouteonsis*) can be found. Common inhabitants of the reefs include butterfly fish, angel fish, parrot fish, stingrays, Blacktip Shark, groupers and cowries. In areas with high turbidity, seaweeds of the genera *Sargassum* and *Turbinaria* dominate, whilst sea worms and crabs are the commonest fauna. The intertidal zone, along rocky shorelines, is habitat for sea fans, oysters, clams and mussels. In January and February shoals of cuttlefish gather to mate in the waters of Ang Thong.

Walks in the Woods

On the islands of Sam Sao and Wua Talab several paths climb through evergreen and mixed deciduous forest to viewpoints that provide panoramic vistas of the curiously shaped islands in a cerulean sea. Sunrise and sunset provide unforgettable views and the best chances of spotting wildlife. A speciality of the islands is a species of lady's slipper orchid (*Paphiopedilum niveum*), which grows nowhere else in the world. It produces beautiful white flowers with purple spots in September. Forest animals include Dusky Langur, Common Wild Pig, monitor lizards and otters. Of the more than 40 bird species that occur within the park, the most noticeable include White-rumped Shama, pigeons, kingfishers and several gull species.

For many years Ang Thong was under the jurisdiction of the Royal Thai Navy, which protected the islands from the sort of ill-considered tourism development that has degraded most other coastal areas around the Gulf of Thailand. Probably the greatest threats to the park are increasing water pollution and increasing numbers of tourist boats damaging the corals with their anchors. However, provided that calls for hotel development within the park can be resisted, it should remain the least spoilt marine park in the Gulf of Thailand.

SIRINATH MARINE NATIONAL PARK

Turtle Beach and a Fringing Coral Reef

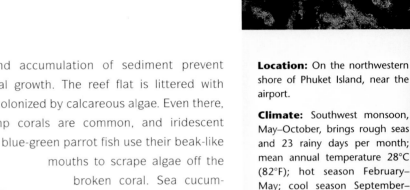

Sirinath Marine National Park was established in the northwest corner of the famous resort island of Phuket to protect two beaches and a coral reef. Mai Khao Beach is the longest and least-developed beach on Phuket, whilst to its south, Nai Yang Beach is fringed by the island's largest coral reef. The park was originally established in 1981 under a different name, Had Nai Yang National Park. It now covers 22 square kilometres (8½ square miles) of land and 68 square kilometres (26 square miles) of coastal waters. Although not the grandest reef in Thailand, the park provides one of the most accessible introductions to coral ecology.

The Fringing Reef

Starting directly from Nai Yang Beach, the fringing reef can provide hours of fascinating exploration for anyone with a snorkel and mask. More than 200 coral species have been recorded in the park. Fringing reefs gradually spread seawards from gently sloping tropical beaches. Swimming out from the beach, snorkellers first pass over the reef flat or back reef. Here, reduced water

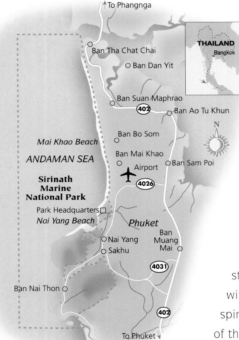

Above, right: *Solitary mushroom corals, some up to 30 cm across, litter the reef flat at Nai Yang Beach.*

circulation and accumulation of sediment prevent extensive coral growth. The reef flat is littered with coral rubble, colonized by calcareous algae. Even there, however, hump corals are common, and iridescent blue-green parrot fish use their beak-like mouths to scrape algae off the broken coral. Sea cucumbers, sea urchins and mushroom corals, the latter looking just like upturned mushroom caps, are scattered across the seabed. Mushroom corals are able to clear away sediment from their upper surfaces, so are able to thrive amongst the debris of the back reef.

Swimmers should beware of stripy brown-and-white lion fish with their flamboyant fins and spines. Venom in glands at the base of the spines is highly toxic.

Farther out towards the reef crest, approximately 1.5 kilometres (1 mile) offshore, more living corals are encountered. Most of the dominant reef-forming corals, including *Acropora*, *Porites*, and *Montastrea*, can be seen. Massive brain corals and spine corals are the most developed. The reef crest is the most actively growing part of the reef. There, waves oxygenate the water and keep the corals clear of sediment. Spurs or buttresses extend to the edge of the reef, with surge channels in between. Along the reef edge, Black-tip Reef Sharks are occasionally seen.

Location: On the northwestern shore of Phuket Island, near the airport.

Climate: Southwest monsoon, May–October, brings rough seas and 23 rainy days per month; mean annual temperature 28°C (82°F); hot season February–May; cool season September–December.

When to Go: December to April.

Access: By car from Phuket City, head 25 kilometres (16 miles) north on Highway 402. The turnoff for the airport (Highway 4031) continues to the national park. Pickup-truck taxis (*song taew*) can be hired from Phuket City to the national park.

Permits: None required.

Equipment: Sunblock is essential, or wear a tee-shirt when snorkelling; swimming and snorkelling equipment.

Facilities: Park bungalows, a dormitory, tents for rent and a restaurant at the park headquarters; resorts at the southern end of Nai Yang Beach; a visitor centre at Mai Khao.

Watching Wildlife: Coral-reef life: soft and hard corals, sea anemones, reef fish, sharks, sea turtles.

Visitor Activities: Relaxing on beaches; swimming and snorkelling.

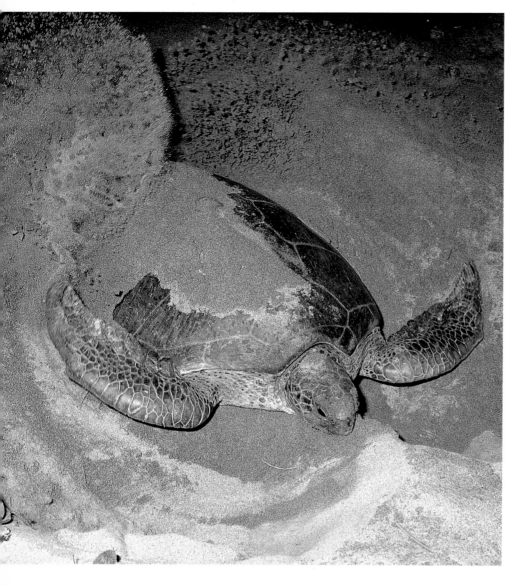

Swimmers exploring the reef from the beach should be aware of the tides, taking care to return to the beach before the receding tide makes it impossible to swim above the coral.

Turtle Conservation

Sirinath is probably the last place on Phuket where sea turtles still nest. Tourism development has not been kind to these magnificent marine reptiles. Their nests are trampled on tourist beaches or their eggs collected for sale as a delicacy, whilst offshore they choke on plastic bags, mistaking them for jellyfish, their favourite food. These factors have all but extirpated nesting sea turtles from Phuket's beaches. At Mai Khao Beach, however, in the north of the marine park, local villagers have been working to conserve sea turtles, particularly the Leatherback Turtle, for more than a decade. In 1991 the villagers organized themselves into a turtle conservation group with the help of Wildlife Fund Thailand and the Phuket Environmental Conservation Club. During the nesting season (November to February), volunteers patrol the beaches to deter egg thieves. Whenever females lay eggs in an unsuitable location, such as where seawater can drown the nest, the volunteers relocate the eggs to safer sites. In the first year of the project only one nest was found, but 10 years later villagers were locating up to 20 nests each year. In addition to Leatherbacks, three other turtle species – Pacific Ridley, Hawksbill and Green – also occur in the marine park.

The Pressures for Mass Tourism

Being the last unspoilt sandy beaches on such a famously over-developed holiday island has created an almost irresistible pressure to allow hotel construction. Until recently a resort built at the south of Nai Yang Beach openly boasted in advertisements that it was located inside the national park. The national park has now been renamed and redefined, following uncertainty over the location of its original boundaries. The threat of further tourism development on these pristine and eco-logically critical beaches is, however, bound to continue.

Above, left: *Female Green Turtles dig their nests on sandy beaches laying up to 100 eggs. Unfortunately the eggs are a delicacy and egg collectors raid many nests.*

Left: *Two months after egg laying, hatchlings emerge at night and dash for the sea. They head for areas of sea grasses, which are their main food.*

Left: *The best coral is found along the leading edge of a fringing reef, the most actively growing part of the reef.*

Below, left: *The Lion Fish or Winged Fire Fish is one of the most venomous of fish. Its spines act like hypodermic needles injecting poison into enemies from glands at the base of the spines.*

Below: *Large white spots help distinguish the Clown Triggerfish from other species. Found amongst reefs in the Andaman Sea, it is a popular aquarium fish.*

TARUTAO MARINE NATIONAL PARK

Southeast Asia's Largest Marine Preserve

Tarutao Marine National Park was declared in 1974 to protect forested islands, coral reefs and sea-turtle nesting beaches off the western coast of Satun Province in southwest Thailand. With an area of 1,490 square kilometres (575 square miles), of which 84 per cent is ocean, it is Southeast Asia's largest marine preserve. The park is home to at least 869 vascular plant species, 30 mammals, 142 birds and 57 butterfly species.

The park features three island groups. Ko Tarutao, the largest island, reaches a maximum elevation of 708 metres (2,322 feet) above sea level. The Ko Rawi–Ko Adang island group lies about 50 kilometres (31 miles) west of Tarutao. The shore of one of the smaller islands, Ko Hin Ngam, is covered with

polished pebbles. Local people believe that the spirit of Ko Hin Ngam will curse anyone who removes a stone. Midway between the two island groups lies a tiny cluster of islands, of which Ko Kai and Ko Klang are the largest.

Forests

Most of Ko Tarutao and the larger surrounding islands are covered with dense mixed deciduous forest, with evergreen forest along stream valleys. Trees of the families *Dipterocarpaceae*, *Leguminosae*, *Meliaceae* and *Anacardiaceae* form a closed canopy at 30–40 metres (98–131 feet). Palm trees, fig trees, woody climbers and epiphytes create an equatorial atmosphere. Other minor terrestrial habitats include scrub and heath, freshwater swamps and marshes, beach vegetation and coastal heath forest.

About 7,000–8,500 years ago, as sea levels rose at the end of the last ice age, populations of Red Giant Flying Squirrel, Bush-tailed Porcupine, Dusky Langur, Lesser Mouse Deer and Malayan Flying Lemur became isolated on Ko Tarutao and have since evolved into distinct subspecies. Other mammals, commonly seen, include Common Wild Pig and Long-tailed Macaque. Forest birds include Oriental Pied Hornbill, Green Imperial Pigeon and Blue-winged Pitta. Wildlife is most

The map shows: To Ban Pak Bara; THAILAND, Bangkok; ANDAMAN SEA; Tarutao Marine National Park; Park Headquarters, Pante Malaca Bay, Waterfall, Son Bay, Waterfall, Ko Tarutao, Talo Wao Bay; Ko Adang; Ko Kai; Ko Klang; Makham Bay; Ko Rang Nok; Talo-Ou-Dang Bay; Waterfall, Ko Rawi; Ko Rong; Waterfall; Ko Hin Ngam; MALAYSIA

Opposite, top: *Rugged coastal scenery and dense forest are combined at Tarutao Marine National Park.*

Opposite, below left: *The Angelfish or Round Batfish is found throughout the Gulf of Thailand and the Andaman Sea.*

Opposite, below right: *Malayan Flying Lemurs can glide up to 100 m between trees on membranes stretched between their legs. Helpless on the ground, they are totally arboreal.*

Above, right: *The Mangrove Snake is often found on branches overhanging water.*

Location: 40 km (25 miles) northwest of the provincial capital of Satun, 22 km (14 miles) out to sea from Pak Bara.

Climate: Heavy seas during May–October monsoon; violent storms any time of year; annual rainfall 2,614 mm (103 in); mean temperature 27°C (81°F) November–December, rising to 28°C (82°F) March–April.

When to Go: December to April.

Access: Daily public boats or chartered boats from Pak Bara to Ko Tarutao and Ko Adang.

Permits: None required. Closed during the monsoon. Open mid-November to mid-May, weather permitting. During the closed season, park staff cannot assist visitors stranded on islands. Prospective visitors should telephone the park office at Pak Bara (074 781285 or 074 729002-3).

Equipment: Light clothing, boots, swimming gear, sunblock, insect repellent, torch, snorkel or scuba equipment. Re-usable water bottles.

Facilities: Bungalows sleeping two to four people for rent on Ko Tarutao and Ko Adang (advanced booking advised); village accommodation on Ko Lipe; information centres and restaurants at Pak Bara, Ko Tarutao and Ko Adang; guide trails on Ko Tarutao and Ko Adang; snorkelling equipment for hire.

Watching Wildlife: Seabirds, marine mammals, coral reefs, fish.

Visitor Activities: Birdwatching, scuba diving and snorkelling, visiting Sea Gypsies.

easily observed on the walk from the park headquarters to Ao Son Beach. A leaflet about the walk is available from the park office.

Intertidal Habitats

The beaches provide nesting sites for four sea-turtle species: Pacific Ridley, Hawksbill, Green and Leatherback. Unfortunately, sea-turtle populations have declined dramatically because of egg collecting and hunting. Female turtles haul up on the beaches to lay their eggs at night from October to April. Visitors lucky enough to witness these rare events should inform the park staff, so that nests can be protected from egg collectors and marauding Common Wild Pigs.

Perhaps the most interesting intertidal habitat is mangrove forest, dominated by *Rhizophora*, *Sonneratia*, *Bruguiera* and *Ceriops* trees. From the park headquarters, boats take visitors through mangrove forest, up the Pante Malaca stream, to a short boardwalk that leads to Crocodile Cave. Trained park rangers introduce visitors to mangrove wildlife, including fiddler crabs and remarkable mudskipper fish, which can survive out of water. Along the river, Brahminy Kites dive for food, along with occasional White-bellied Sea-eagles.

Another coastal feature not to be missed is a spectacular natural stone archway on a beautiful white sandy beach on Ko Kai.

Coral Reefs and the Open Ocean

Tarutao has been described as Southeast Asia's 'last frontier' for scuba divers because, despite the park's rich reef fauna, no live-on-board dive companies operate there. Scuba divers must bring their own equipment, although snorkels are available for hire. The best sites for reef enthusiasts are around the outer islands of Rawi, Adang, Lipe and Hin Ngam. The reefs are composed of 140 hard and soft coral species and are home to more than 140 fish species. Among many species, divers can see sharks, rays, eels, catfish, angel fish, butterfly fish, anemone fish, sponges and possibly Hawksbill and Green Turtles.

When travelling around the park by boat, visitors can occasionally see Dolphins. Sittang Whales sometimes pass through the park and Dugongs are probably still resident, although sightings are rare.

Sea Gypsies

About 500 Sea Gypsies, known locally as *chao leh*, live on Ko Lipe, having originally settled there about 100 years ago. They are of Indo-Malay descent and traditionally migrated between islands, fishing and collecting shellfish and lobsters. On Ko Lipe they also provide very simple accommodation and boat services for tourists. They have their own language and religion, which involves the worship of sea spirits.

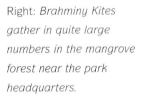

Right: *Brahminy Kites gather in quite large numbers in the mangrove forest near the park headquarters.*

Above: *When cruising among the islands, visitors should keep a sharp look out for dolphins, which are occasionally seen in Tarutao's waters.*

Left: *The Blue-spotted Fantail Ray lives on sand seabeds particularly around coral reefs.*

Paradise in Danger

Tarutao faces serious ecological problems. Garbage, mostly plastic bottles, accumulating along the high-tide lines, creates an eyesore and a hazard to wildlife. Most of it does not originate from the park, but is washed out from the mainland or thrown from boats. Visitors are asked to help to recycle garbage in the park and take their own rubbish to the mainland when they leave. Another unwelcome development is the upgrading of the track that runs the length of Ko Tarutao into a surfaced road. Easier access for motor vehicles will increase disturbance of wildlife in the island's interior.

Prisoners and Pirates

The serenity of Ko Tarutao today belies the island's grim history. In 1936 prisons were constructed on the island, and by 1941 3,000 convicts were incarcerated there. Sharks and crocodiles infested the coastal waters, deterring escape. Tragedy struck during World War II, when supplies of food and medicine to the prisons were cut off. More than 700 convicts and guards died from starvation and malaria. In desperation, several prisoners and guards raided a passing merchant ship. Finding wealth beyond their dreams, they became notorious pirates. The plunder continued until 1946, when the British Navy restored law and order and the prisons were closed.

Above: *Mangrove forests provide safe roosting sites for fruit bats like this* Macroglossus lagochilus. *During the night, they fly from the mangrove to forage for fruit in terrestrial forest.*

Right: *A dense profusion of many plant forms are typical of the canopy of the forest of the interior of Ko Tarutao.*

Above: *Mudskippers can survive out of water for long periods. Here two males engage in a territorial dispute on a patch of mangrove mud.*

Left: *Useless for feeding, the enormous right claw of this fiddler crab is used for display and to fight rivals. Fiddler crabs and their larvae are one of the most sought after food sources for fish and other marine life.*

THALEBAN NATIONAL PARK

Where Mountains Meet Mangroves

From forested mountains to unspoilt mangrove forest, Thaleban National Park has a wide range of scenic and wildlife attractions. When created in 1980, the park covered just 101 square kilometres (39 square miles) of forested mountains, but a southern extension was later added to include limestone crags and mangrove forest on the Andaman coast. Today, the park covers 196 square kilometres (76 square miles), ranging from sea level to a maximum elevation of 756 metres (2,480 feet) above sea level at the summit of Khao Chin. The park is long and thin in shape and lies between the Thailand–Malaysia border and the main highway linking Hat Yai with Satun. The international border forms the boundary of the park to the south and east for more than 20 kilometres (12 miles). South of the border, Malaysia's new Nakawan State Park adjoins Thaleban, creating an extended

conservation zone totalling 300 square kilometres (115 square miles).

Steep-sided limestone ridges and peaks and more gently rounded granite hills are the main topographic features. In impervious granite areas, waterfalls are common. Yaroy Waterfalls and Don Bliew Waterfalls lie 6 and 10 kilometres (4 and 6 miles), respectively, north of the park headquarters. Several caves occur in the limestone areas, including Don Din Cave, 2 kilometres (1 mile) north of the park headquarters, out of which a multitude of bats emerge at dusk.

Tropical evergreen forest, mixed deciduous forest and mangrove forest are the main vegetation types. Two circular trails (guides required) near the park headquarters lead visitors past massive, buttressed trees up to 50 metres (164 feet) in height, rattan palms, lianas and a wide range of epiphytes, all of which create a distinctly equatorial atmosphere to the evergreen forest.

The park is home to a small band of Sakai tribal people. Now estimated to number fewer than 10, they still live as hunter-gatherers, building temporary shelters of leaves and subsisting on forest products. They may well be descended from the earliest human beings to inhabit Thailand, the so-called Hoabinhians, whose cave sites date back 38,000 years in Krabi Province.

Opposite: Lot Poo You Cave is a limestone archway connecting two stretches of beautiful mangrove forest in the southern part of the national park.

Above, right: The Jambu Fruit-dove is a scarce resident at Thaleban.

Location: Extreme southwest of peninsular Thailand, about 40 km (25 miles) northeast of the provincial capital, Satun.

Climate: Mostly hot and humid; mean annual temperature 27–28°C (81–82°F), slightly hotter in April and cooler in November–December; mean annual rainfall 2,600 mm (79 in); very wet during southwest monsoon (May–October); slightly drier December–March.

When to Go: Avoid the monsoon season. Best birdwatching is from November to March.

Access: Shared pickup-truck taxi from Satun market hourly to the park headquarters. Public buses from Satun or Hat Yai along Highway 406 to Khuan Sataw. From there motorcycle taxis to the park headquarters, 9 km (6 miles) along Highway 4184. Rental cars from Hat Yai.

Permits: None required. Telephone 01-230056 to arrange your visit.

Equipment: Light forest wear and walking boots; sunscreen and torch; mosquito repellent and a mosquito net, protection against leeches.

Facilities: Ten bungalows, sleeping 3 to 14 persons, campsite, small visitor centre, restaurant, forest trails with guides available.

Watching Wildlife: Primates, hornbills, birds of prey, Serow; plants more usually associated with equatorial forest.

Visitor Activities: Birdwatching, forest hikes, botanizing, visiting caves and waterfalls.

Thaleban Lake

The park headquarters has a picturesque setting, in a narrow valley between two steep mountain ridges, beside a marshy lake that provides the park with its name. Thaleban is probably derived from the Malay *leur aud ga ban*, which means a low-lying marshy area. According to a local legend, the valley was once fertile paddy fields, but a violent earthquake struck the area about 300 years ago. The sheer sides of the valley crumbled and dammed the stream, forming a lake, which is gradually filling with silt and becoming a marsh.

One inhabitant of the lake that visitors will be immediately aware of is the amazing, but inappropriately named, Barking Frog, *Rana glandulosa*. This amphibian possesses disproportionally large throat sacs, with which it produces a very loud call – not at all like a barking dog – more like 'Woaaahp! Woaaahp!'. Around the lake, patient observers will see Asian Paradise-flycatcher, Common Kingfisher and Green-crested Lizard.

Primates and Other Mammals

One of the park's main attractions for wildlife enthusiasts is the ease with which primates can be viewed. Around the park headquarters Dusky Langurs and Long-tailed Macaques are easily seen. Although by no means tame, they are partially habituated to human visitors, providing excellent opportunities for photography. Visitors who stay overnight will undoubtedly be roused by the songs of numerous families of White-handed Gibbons, proclaiming their territories all around the park headquarters. Visitors who walk quietly along forest trails early in the morning can be rewarded with sightings of these delightful animals. Whilst watching for primates, Black Giant Squirrels are also seen easily. Lesser Mouse Deer and Common Wild Pig are both common, Serows haunt the limestone crags, and Malayan Tapir and Malayan Sun Bear are present, but very elusive.

Birds of Prey – Migration Spectacle

Another wildlife attraction is an extraordinary biannual migration of thousands of birds of prey. The mountain ridges on either side of the park headquarters are used by the birds as landmarks to guide their flight south into Malaysia during October and November, and north again into Thailand during March and April. Visitors are recommended to settle themselves at the small cafés near the border post early in the morning and scan the ridge tops with binoculars. During the migration seasons, hundreds of buzzards, eagles, sparrowhawks and bazas can be seen passing by in just a few hours.

The park boasts no fewer than eight hornbill species. Rare bird species include the Great Argus pheasant and the Narcissus Flycatcher. More easily seen species include Red Junglefowl, Thick-billed Pigeon, Vernal Hanging Parrot, Coppersmith Barbet and Great Iora. A total of 289 bird species has been recorded.

Left: *Looking remarkably like a dried up leaf, this Horned Toad achieves almost perfect camouflage on the forest floor.*

Overleaf: *Dawn over forested mountains.*

Below: *The marshy lake, after which the national park is named, provides an attractive feature near the park headquarters. This is the habitat of Thaleban's most vocal resident, the Barking Frog.*

A Boat Ride through Mangroves to a Hidden Cave

A long-tailed boat can be hired from Tammalang Pier, about 9 kilometres (6 miles) south of Satun, for trips to Lot Poo You Cave, in the south of the park. After crossing an estuary, the boat enters a maze of meandering channels through mangrove forest as it approaches precipitous limestone cliffs that plunge into the sea. The dominant tree genera here are *Rhizophora* and *Bruguiera*. Birds likely to be seen along the way include Brahminy Kite, Common Flameback and Black-capped Kingfisher. On mud banks, colourful fiddler crabs and amphibious mudskipper fish are easily seen. The short cave, Lot Poo You, provides the climax of the trip. The boat glides right through a sheer limestone cliff, emerging into an equally attractive stretch of mangrove forest on the other side.

Although the mangrove forest is in good condition, strenuous efforts are being made to repair damaged areas. A mangrove-tree nursery near Tammalang Pier produces thousands of saplings for restoration plantings. The planted areas appear to be thriving.

SUMMARY OF CONSERVATION AREAS

The following is a brief summary of all the conservation areas covered in this book, plus a selection of the many national parks that could not be included owing to lack of space. Contact the Royal Forest Department (see address on page 172) for further details.

Central and Southeast Thailand

Chalerm Rattanakosin National Park (59 km²/23 sq miles). Province: Kanchanaburi. Gazetted 1980. Caves and limestone mountains covered with deciduous forest; a historical battleground.

Erawan National Park (550 km²/212 sq miles). Province: Kanchanaburi. Gazetted 1975. The waterfalls are considered the most attractive in Thailand; limestone mountains covered with bamboo deciduous forest; caves containing Stone Age relics.

Kaeng Krachan National Park (2,915 km²/1,125 sq miles). Provinces: Phetchburi and Prachuap Khiri Khan. Gazetted 1981. Extensive evergreen and deciduous forests with a high diversity of mammals and birds; deer, Asian Elephants, bears, and Tigers.

Khao Chamao – Khao Wong National Park (83 km²/32 sq miles). Provinces: Rayong and Chantaburi. Gazetted 1975. The last substantial forest in Rayong; waterfalls, a few large mammals and large numbers of Soro Brook Carp.

Khao Laem National Park (1,497 km²/578 sq miles). Province: Kanchanaburi. Gazetted 1991. Dense forest with gibbons, hornbills and pheasants; a large reservoir that can be explored by boat.

Khao Laem Ya – Mu Ko Samet Marine National Park (131 km²/50 sq miles). Province: Rayong. Gazetted 1981. Fine white sandy beaches, with small patches of coral reef just off shore, showcasing marine life of the Gulf of Thailand.

Khao Sam Roi Yot Marine National Park (98 km²/38 sq miles). Province: Prachuab Khiri Khan. Gazetted 1966. Striking coastal scenery with huge limestone caves, and one of the most important coastal marshlands for birds in Southeast Asia.

Mu Ko Chang Marine National Park (650 km²/253 sq miles). Province: Trat. Gazetted 1982. The finest dive site in the Gulf of Thailand, with sunken battleships and coral reefs.

Pang Sida National Park (844 km²/326 sq miles). Provinces: Prachinburi. Gazetted 1982. Waterfalls and rock formations. Freshwater crocodile may still survive; more than 200 bird species.

Sai Yok National (500 km²/193 sq miles). Province: Kanchanaburi. Gazetted 1980. Limestone karstland with caves that are home to the world's smallest bat species. Wildlife includes gibbons, monkeys, deer and a few Asian Elephants. Relics from World War II.

Srinakarin National Park (1,534 km²/592 sq miles). Province: Kanchanaburi. Gazetted 1981. Reservoir, waterfalls and a large cave containing a towering Buddha statue. Karen villages provide a cultural attraction.

Thung Yai Naresuan–Huay Kha Khaeng Wildlife Sanctuaries and World Heritage Site (6,427 km²/2,481 sq miles). Provinces: Kanchanaburi, Uthai Thani and Tak. Gazetted 1974. Thailand's most important site for the conservation of large mammals, especially wild cattle, Asian Elephants, and large cats. Not open to the general public; tourism is discouraged.

Northern Thailand

Doi Inthanon National Park (482 km²/186 sq miles). Province: Chiang Mai. Gazetted 1972. Thailand's highest mountain with unique forest and sphagnum bog. Endemic fauna includes subspecies of shrew and sunbird. Regarded as Thailand's best birdwatching site.

Doi Khuntan National Park (255 km²/98 sq miles). Provinces: Lampang and Lampoon. Gazetted 1975. An historic railway tunnel through a mountain, supporting a diversity of forest types with orchids, bamboos, gingers and figs.

Doi Suthep-Pui National Park (261 km²/101 sq miles). Province: Chiang Mai. Gazetted 1981. A forested, montane setting for one of the most revered Buddhist temples in Thailand. An excellent site for birdwatchers, botanists, and visitors seeking a spiritual experience.

Khlong Lan National Park (300 km²/116 sq miles). Province: Kamphaeng Phet. Gazetted 1982. Magnificent waterfalls, rapids and riverine scenery provide a variety of aquatic attractions.

Mae Ping National Park (1,003 km²/387 sq miles). Provinces: Lampoon, Tak and Chiang Mai. Gazetted 1981. The Ping River glides through spectacular limestone cliffs, surrounded by some of the most intact deciduous forest in the north.

Mae Wong National Park (894 km²/345 sq miles). Provinces: Kamphaeng Phet and Nakhon Sawan. Gazetted 1987. An old teak-logging concession undergoing forest recovery. Cool evergreen forest with hornbills and primates.

Mae Yom National Park (455 km²/176 sq miles). Provinces: Lampang and Phrae. Gazetted 1985. One of the last and most important teak forests in Thailand; river islands, rapids and pools.

Nam Nao National Park (990 km²/386 sq miles). Province: Phetchabun. Gazetted 1972. Pine-dipterocarp forest, retaining populations of Asian Elephants, deer, monkeys, gibbons and bears.

Nam Tok Mae Surin National Park (397 km²/153 sq miles). Provinces: Mae Hongson. One of Thailand's tallest waterfalls, splendid views over misty valleys, and a chance to visit hill-tribe villages.

Ob Luang National Park (553 km²/213 sq miles). Province: Chiang Mai. Gazetted 1991. This park offers an imaginary journey back to the Stone Age with the aid of archaeological relics and cliff paintings.

Phu Hin Rong Kla National Park (307 km²/118 sq miles). Provinces: Phitsanuloke, Loei and Phetchabun. Gazetted 1984. A rugged mountain with sheer cliffs and unusual rock formations covered in orchids, ferns and lichens. The site of a bloody battle against Communist insurgents.

Ramkhamhaeng National Park (341 km²/131 sq miles). Province: Sukothai. Gazetted 1980. A forested mountain with spectacular views over the birthplace of Thai culture. Excellent birdwatching and historical relics provide interest for both naturalists and history buffs.

Srilanna National Park (1,406 km²/543 sq miles). Province: Chiang Mai. Gazetted 1989. Boat trips on a placid reservoir and long-distance forest treks to caves and waterfalls.

Sri Satchanalai National Park (213 km²/82 sq miles). Province: Sukothai. Gazetted 1981. Medium-sized, forested hills support more than 70 bird species and a small number of Asian Elephants. Caves and waterfalls are scenic attractions with 13th- to 15th-century ruins nearby.

Thung Salaeng Luang National Park (1,262 km²/487 sq miles). Provinces: Phitsanuloke and Phetchabun. Gazetted 1963. Extensive meadows, dotted with pine trees provide an abundance of wildflowers and grazing for large ungulates. A thunderous waterfall, and caves.

Northeastern Thailand (Isaan)

Khao Yai National Park (2,168 km²/836 sq miles). Provinces: Saraburi, Prachinburi, Nakhon Ratchasima and Nakhon Nayok. Gazetted 1962. Thailand's oldest park, with highly visible wildlife. The best place in Thailand to see Asian Elephants, deer, monkeys, gibbons and hornbills.

Phu Kradung National Park (348 km²/134 sq miles). Province: Loei. Gazetted 1962. A rolling open plateau, studded with pine trees, supporting an unusual flora, including orchids, gentians, gingers and carnivorous plants, reached via a mountain trek.

Phu Pan National Park (666 km²/257 sq miles). Provinces: Kalasin and Sakhon Nakhon. Gazetted 1972. A refuge for World War II resistance fighters and Communist insurgents; a royal palace; waterfalls and rock formations are the main attractions.

Phu Rua National Park (121 km²/47 sq miles). Province: Loei. Gazetted 1979. A sandstone mountain, with natural rockeries smothered in rhododendrons and orchids. Sweeping views, delicate waterfalls and strange rock formations.

Phu Wiang National Park (325 km²/125 sq miles). Province: Khon Kaen. Gazetted 1991. An imaginary visit to the Dinosaur Age; visits to fossil excavation sites and an informative exhibition.

Thap Lan National Park (2,235 km²/863 sq miles). Provinces: Nakhon Ratchasima and Prachinburi. Gazetted 1981. Lowland forests, supporting significant populations of ungulates, primates and large cats, and a great diversity of bird species.

Southern Thailand

Ao Phangnga Marine National Park (400 km²/154 sq miles). Provinces: Krabi and Phangnga. Gazetted 1981. Thailand's most spectacular coastal scenery, with limestone cliffs towering above the ocean. Caves with archaeological relics and rock paintings. Sea canoeing and rock climbing for the adventurous.

Had Nopparat Thara – Mu Ko Phi Phi Marine National Park (390 km²/151 sq miles). Province: Krabi. Gazetted 1983. Tropical islands spoilt by tourism development, but still retaining spectacular scenery and significant seabird populations.

Khao Luang National Park (570 km²/220 sq miles). Province: Nakhon Si Thammarat. Gazetted 1974. The highest mountain in southern Thailand, with tropical rainforest providing habitat for deer, monkeys, Leopards and Tigers, and hornbills.

Khao Panom Bencha National Park (50 km²/19 sq miles). Province: Krabi. Gazetted 1981. Limestone caves and waterfalls surrounded by rainforest with a high diversity of wildlife; deer, gibbons, Leopard, Tiger, pheasants, pittas and hornbills.

Khao Sok National Park (739 km²/285 sq miles). Province: Surat Thani. Gazetted 1980. Giant parasitic flowers, Rafflesia, and rare palm trees in a luxuriant tropical rainforest. A reservoir, which devastated the ecology of the area, now provides recreational opportunities for visitors.

Mu Ko Phetra Marine National Park (494 km²/191 sq miles). Province: Satun. Gazetted 1984. Fine beaches, caves and spectacular cliffs with sculptured rock formations. A shallow bay with rapids cascading into the sea, and coral reefs. A sea-turtle nesting beach.

Mu Ko Ang Thong Marine National Park (102 km²/39 sq miles). Province: Surat Thani. Gazetted 1980. A saltwater lagoon inside an island, colourful coral reefs. Steep forest trails offer views over a scattered archipelago of limestone islets.

Mu Ko Surin Marine National Park (135 km²/52 sq miles). Province: Phangnga. Gazetted 1981. Widely regarded as Thailand's best dive site for coral reefs and associated fauna especially Whale Sharks, sea turtles and Manta Rays. The rare Nicobar Pigeon and a wide variety of seabirds attract ornithologists.

Sirinath Marine National Park (90 km²/35 sq miles). Province: Phuket. Gazetted 1981. One of the most accessible coral reefs for snorkellers, and a nesting beach for sea turtles protected by local villagers.

Tarutao Marine National Park (1,490 km²/575 sq miles). Province: Satun. Gazetted 1974. The largest marine park in Southeast Asia. Sea-turtle nesting beaches, and coral reefs. Island forests with endemic mammal subspecies.

Thaan Bok Koranee National Park (104 km²/40 sq miles). Province: Krabi. Gazetted 1998. Boat rides and forest walks to waterfalls and caves with prehistoric remains.

Thaleban National Park (196 km²/76 sq miles). Province: Satun. Gazetted 1980. A small but diverse park, featuring evergreen forest with an equatorial atmosphere, a marshy lake and extensive mangroves. Hornbills and migrating raptors attract birdwatchers.

Useful Addresses

Biodiversity Research and Training Program
15th Floor Gypsum Tower
539/2 Sri Ayuthaya Road
Rajdhavee
Bangkok 10400
tel: 02 642 5322
fax: 02 642 5163
e-mail: brt@brtprogram.org

Bird Conservation Society of Thailand
(Formerly the Bangkok Bird Club)
69/12 Ramindra 24
Joorakheabua, Ladprao
Bangkok 10400
tel: 02 943 5956
fax: 02 519 3385
e-mail: bcst@box1.a-net.net.th

Chiang Mai University Herbarium and Forest Restoration Research Unit
Department of Biology
Faculty of Science
Chiang Mai University
Chiang Mai, 50200
tel: 053 943346 or 943358
fax: 053 892259
e-mail: scopplrn@chiangmai.ac.th

Conservation Data Centre
Institute of Science and Technology
for Research and Development
Mahidol University
Salaya
Nakhon Pathom, 73170

Hornbill Research Foundation
c/o Department of Microbiology
Faculty of Science
Mahidol University
Rama 6 Road
Bangkok 10400
tel: 02 246 0063 ext. 4606
fax: 02 246 3026

Oriental Bird Club
c/o The Lodge
Sandy
Bedfordshire SG19 2DL
England
e-mail: mail@orientalbirdclub.org

Royal Forest Department
61 Phaholyothin Road
Ladprao
Chatuchak
Bangkok 10900
tel: 02 579 5734
fax: 02 579 9576

Seub Nakhasathien Foundation
50 Phaholyothin Road
Bangkok 10900
tel: 02 561 2469
fax: 02 561 2470

The Western Forest Elephant Conservation Project
37 Moo 8, Tambon Kaeng Sian
Amphoe Muang
Kanchanburi 71000
tel: (034) 624684
e-mail: elenet@vip.ksc.net.th

Wildlife Fund Thailand
251/88-90 Phaholyothin Road
Bangkhen
Bangkok 10220
tel: 02 521 3435
fax: 02 552 6083
e-mail: WILDLIFE@mozart.inet.co.th

World Wide Fund for Nature Thailand Programme
104 Outreach Building
AIT
PO Box 4 Klong Luang
Pathumtani, 12120
tel: 02 524 6128-9
fax: 02 524 6134

Further Reading

Banziger, H. (1991) Stench and fragrance: unique pollination lure of Thailand's largest flower, *Rafflesia kerrii* Meijer. *Natural History Bulletin of the Siam Society* 39:19-52.

Cox, M. J., van Dijk, P. P., Nabhitabhata, J., and Thirakhupt, K. (1998) *A Photographic Guide to Snakes and Other Reptiles of Thailand and South-East Asia*. New Holland Publishers, London.

Ecological Research Department, (1993) *Endangered Species and Habitats of Thailand*. Thailand Institute of Scientific and Technological Research in collaboration with Wildlife Fund Thailand, Bangkok.

Gardner, S., Sidisunthorn, P., and Anusarnsunthorn, V. (2000) *A Field Guide to the Forest Trees of Northern Thailand*. Kobfai Publishing Project, Bangkok.

Graham, M., and Round, P. (1994) *Thailand's Vanishing Flora and Fauna*. Finance One Public Company, Bangkok.

Grassman, L. I., Jr., (1999) Ecology and behaviour of the Indochinese Leopard in Kaeng Krachan National Park, Thailand. *Natural History Bulletin of the Siam Society* 47: 77-93.

Gray, D., Piprell, C., and Graham, M. (1994) *National Parks of Thailand* (revised edn). Industrial Finance Corporation of Thailand, Bangkok.

Henley, T. (1996) *Waterfalls and Gibbon Calls, Exploring Khao Sok National Park*. Thom Henley, Phuket.

Henley, T. (1999) *Reef to Rainforests, Mountains to Mangroves, A Guide to South Thailand's Natural Wonders*. Dawn of Happiness Resort Co., Krabi.

Higham, C., and Thosarat, R. (1998) *Prehistoric Thailand From Early Settlement to Sukothai*. River Books, Bangkok.

Humphrey, S. R., and Bain, J. R. (1990) *Endangered Animals of Thailand*. Sandhill Crane Press, Florida, USA.

Hutcharern, C., and Tubtim, N. (1995). *Checklist of Forest Insects in Thailand* (vol. 1). Office of Environmental Policy and Planning, Bangkok.

Kekule, L. B. (1999) *Wildlife in the Kingdom of Thailand*. Asia Books, Bangkok.

Lees, P. (1999) *The Dive Sites of Thailand*. Asia Books, Bangkok.

Lekagul, B., and McNeely, J. A. (1988) *Mammals of Thailand* (2nd edn). Saha Karn Bhaet Co. Ltd, Bangkok.

Lekagul, B., and Round, P. D. (1991) *A Guide to the Birds of Thailand*. Saha Karn Bhaet Co. Ltd, Bangkok.

Majchacheep, S. (1989) *Marine Animals of Thailand*. Prae Pittaya Publishers, Bangkok.

Nutaphand, W. (1979) *The Turtles of Thailand*. Siamfarm Zoological Garden, Bangkok.

Pinratana, A. (1979) *Butterflies in Thailand* (vols. 1-6). Viratham Press, Bangkok.

Pinratana, A., and Lampe, R.E.J. (1990) *Moths of Thailand*. Viratham Press, Bangkok.

Robson, C. (2000). *A Field Guide to the Birds of Thailand and South-East Asia*. New Holland Publishers, London.

Stewart-Cox, B., and Cubitt, G. (1995) *Wild Thailand*. Asia Books, Bangkok.

INDEX

Acknowledgements

The information presented in this book was derived from park officials of the Royal Forest Department, references listed at the back of this book and from the author's own observations during visits to the parks. The author is grateful to many individuals who generously contributed their time and knowledge during the writing of this book. During fieldwork, many Royal Forest Department Officers assisted. They are thanked for their guidance and hospitality, particularly Samloay Boonmah, Nan Chalernkuhn, Kanokwan Monmoa, Siradat Boonmak Chalerm Wonglom, Sanchai Longthung, Preecha Thongjaem, Songran Gaewlah, Bumrong Hortsaisong and Anirut Madween.

Many of the brief lists of birds or mammals included in each park description were derived from the Conservation Data Centre of Mahidol University, under the direction of Warren Brockelman and Philip D. Round. Parts or all of the text were reviewed by Kevin Woods, David Blakesley, Smansnid Svasti, Belinda Stewart-Cox, Bruce Kekule, Arthur Wright, Martin Greijmans, Maria Hardy and Martin van de Bult. The author is grateful for their useful comments, advice and encouragement. J. F. Maxwell provided several plant names and botanical advice. Sudarat Zangkum, Thanawat Dorkmaihom and Woravit Rattanakit are thanked for their help with translation of information from Thai into English. The Biology Department of Chiang Mai University is acknowledged for institutional support of the author over many years, providing him with the opportunity to visit and study many of the parks described in this book.

Photographer's Acknowledgements

The Royal Forest Department. Seub Nakhasathien Foundation. Phornthep Phornprapha, President, Think Earth/Siam Motors Co. Ltd. Dr Schwann Tunhikorn, Sumonta Nakornthab and Chalermlap Ganachara na Ayudhaya, Tourism Authority of Thailand. Shangri-la Hotel, Bangkok. Belinda Stewart-Cox, Dr John Dransfield (Royal Botanic Gardens, Kew), Alan Guignon, Dr Roy Watling (Royal Botanic Garden, Edinburgh).

Also a special thanks to my wife, Janet, who has accompanied me on all my travels in Thailand and has been a constant source of encouragement and inspiration.

Photographic Acknowledgements

The author, the publishers and the principal photographer extend their thanks to the following who generously loaned their photographs for inclusion in this book.

Michael AW: p54 (br), p148 (t, b), p154 (b), p157 (t)

Hans Banziger: p34 (t), p38 (tl, tr), p64 (t), p67 (t), p71 (b), p81, p82 (b), p96 (r), p97 (b), p121(t), p126 (bl), p129, p138 (br), p162 (t), p167 (t)

Chris Caldicott/Axiom: p98 (t)

Gerald Cubitt: p2-3, p4-5, p6-7, p8-9, p10, p11, p12, p13, p14, p15, p18, p19, p20, p21, p22, p23 (b), p24, p25, p26, p27, p28, p29, p30 (tl, tr), p31 (t), p32 (bl), p33, p34 (b), p35 (t), p36 (bl, br), p39, p40 (b), p41, p42 (br), p44, p47 (t), p48, p49, p50, p51, p53, p54 (bl), p55, p59 (bl), p61, p62, p64 (b), p65 (t, b), p66 (t), p68 (tl, cl), p72 (cl, bl), p73, p74 (t), p75 (t), p77 (b), p78, p79, p80, p82 (t), p84 (t, br), p85, p86, p88, p89, p90, p92, p93 (tl, b); p94 (tl, cl, br), p97 (t), p100 (b), p102 (b), p103, p104, p106 (t), p107 (br), p108, p109, p110, p111, p112, p114, p115, p117, p118 (t, bl), p122 (t), p124, p125, p126 (br), p127, p128, p130, p131, p132, p133, p134 (cl, r), p136 (b), p139, p140 (b), p142, p144 (t), p145 (t), p146, p147, p149, p153, p156, p158 (br), p160, p163, p164, p165, p166, p168-169

Ron Emmons: p32 (br), p35 (b), p46 (t), p47 (bl, br), p54 (t), p68 (r), p70, p72 (tl, r), p74 (b), p75 (b), p76 (t, b), p77 (t); p83 (t, bl), p94 (r), p100 (t), p118 (br), p120 (tl, b), p121 (b), p134 (tl), p135, p136 (t), p137 (l), p150 (t)

John Everingham: p36 (t), p37, p45, p58 (t), p116, p138 (t, bl), p141 (b), p145 (b), p158 (t), p159, p162 (b)

Chew Yen Fook: p31 (b), p67 (br), p84 (bl), p87, p93 (tr), p95, p98 (bl), p105, p122 (br), p123

Jack Jackson: p46 (b), p56 (t, b), p134 (bl), p136 (cl), p137 (r), p143, p144 (b), p150 (b), P151 (tr, l, br), p154 (c), p155, p157 (bl, br), p158 (bl), p161 (t, b)

Bruce Kekule: p23 (t), p30 (b), p57, p59 (br), p109

Wachara Kireewong/Artasia, Bangkok: p32 (t)

t = top; b = bottom; c = centre; l = left; r = right